THE ULTIMATE
VEGAN
COOKBOOK
FOR YOUR INSTANT POT®

THE ULTIMATE
VEGAN
COOKBOOK
FOR YOUR INSTANT POT®

80 EASY AND DELICIOUS PLANT-BASED RECIPES
THAT YOU CAN MAKE IN HALF THE TIME

KATHY HESTER

BESTSELLING AUTHOR OF *THE EASY VEGAN COOKBOOK* AND *THE GREAT VEGAN BEAN BOOK*

PAGE STREET
PUBLISHING CO.

PAGE STREET
PUBLISHING CO.

First published in 2017 by
Page Street Publishing Co.
27 Congress Street, Suite 105
Salem, MA 01970
www.pagestreetpublishing.com

Distributed by Macmillan, sales in Canada by The Canadian Manda Group.

20 19 18 17   3 4 5

ISBN-13: 978-1-62414-338-0
ISBN-10: 1-62414-338-5

Library of Congress Control Number: 2016941505

Cover and book design by Page Street Publishing Co.
Photography by Kathy Hester

Printed and bound in the United States

Instant Pot® is a registered trademark of Instant Pot Company, which is not associated with this book.

Page Street is proud to be a member of 1% for the Planet. Members donate one percent of their sales to one or more of the over 1,500 environmental and sustainability charities across the globe who participate in this program.

TABLE OF CONTENTS

Everything You Need to Know About Your Instant Pot

A LITTLE ABOUT ME

I'm Kathy Hester and I love my Instant Pot. It's my hope that you'll be joining me in my addiction to it, too. A few years ago I had just finished writing *The Easy Vegan Cookbook* and I rewarded myself with a brand-new, shiny Instant Pot.

The first thing I did was join a few Facebook groups that I mention at the end of this book. I was amazed at just how active and helpful they were. It was wonderful to see how much people were cooking in their Instant Pots. I suggest you join a few, too, for the help and camaraderie. Plus, I may see you there from time to time!

Not long after, I started using my Instant Pot for soups and stews and to cook dried beans from scratch. The more I used it, the more ideas I had for recipes—including layering different dishes in the same Instant Pot to make a complete meal.

There are several reasons to use an Instant Pot. I like the fact there is a lot of hands-off time, like you get using a slow cooker. My friend Jill Nussinow loves pressure cooking in general because of the speed. She tends toward cooking a little longer and releasing the pressure manually, whereas I cook a little less and let the pressure release naturally. The food ends up perfect either way.

You'll find that the Instant Pot will fit into your life quickly and you will wonder how you ever lived without it. One of my favorite things is that the pot you cook in is stainless steel. That makes it easy to clean, and there's no icky coating that can leech into your food.

There are so many options with your Instant Pot, plus you can still slow cook in it. Later in this section I go through all the cooking settings so you'll be in the know. It's a slow cooker, pressure cooker, rice cooker and steamer all in one!

The vegetables and grains tend to be less mushy when you pressure cook versus slow cook, and people with texture issues, like Cheryl, my grown-up picky eater, will enjoy that fact.

In addition to the recipes in this book, you can see more of my recipes at HealthySlowCooking.com, which has all kinds of recipes, including ones for the Instant Pot.

I've also written several other vegan cookbooks, including:

The Vegan Slow Cooker
The Great Vegan Bean Book
Vegan Slow Cooking for Two or Just You
OATrageous Oatmeals
The Easy Vegan Cookbook

I just want to thank you for reading *The Ultimate Vegan Cookbook for Your Instant Pot* and I hope it makes dinner easier!

WHY PRESSURE COOK?

Pressure cooking cooks things in less time. An electric pressure cooker uses mostly hands-off cooking time, and that makes it a winner in my book.

Pressure cooking cuts the cooking time significantly. But you have to remember when you read that it only takes 3 minutes to cook steel-cut oats, we are not counting the time to come up to pressure or the time to release the pressure so you can finally eat your oatmeal. But even though it takes longer than 3 minutes, the oats are still cooked in half the time from start to finish.

I know some of you may be wondering whether I'm giving up slow cooking. The answer is no. I think slow cooking and pressure cooking both make our lives easier. Both have lots of hands-off cooking time and give us a much deserved break. So I'll be doing both for the foreseeable future.

Slow cooking is great if you are more inclined to put together dinner before you go to work. Pressure cooking is very helpful if you like to cook when you get home from work. Either way, you'll be saving tons of money and time eating at home.

I do think that pressure cooking is kinder to vegetables, and it's easier for them to retain a perfect texture. There are ways to layer vegetables in different dishes or wrap in foil so that you can cook two different kinds of veggies to perfection at the same time.

You will find that your Instant Pot is so versatile that you will be using it to cook up quick, last-minute meals, batches of soy yogurt and amazing three-part meals in one pot! The convenience of being able to throw some ingredients into your Instant Pot at the last minute and have a wonderful one-pot meal in less than 30 minutes cannot be beat.

WHAT IS AN INSTANT POT ANYWAY?

Instant Pot® is a brand of electric multi-cooker that happens to do all the things I need to do in the kitchen. It pressure cooks and slow cooks; has a built-in rice cooker, steamer; and can even sauté. The 7-in-1-model even has a yogurt maker setting, too! Not bad for one appliance, right?

I love the idea of having all these things in one. It saves room in the kitchen and for most meals I only have one pot to clean. It saves a ton of work to sauté in the same pan that you will finish your meal in.

Other electric pressure cookers can be used to make these recipes. You may need to make some modifications though, since all of these recipes were only tested in the 6-quart (6-L) Lux or Duo models of the Instant Pot®. Only some were tested in other electric slow cookers. At the time of writing, an 8-quart (8-L) Instant Pot® is being developed; look for the most current information at HealthySlowCooking.com/VeganInstantPot. All of the recipes in this book should still work in the 8-quart (8-L) and larger amounts may be used in addition to the ones suggested for the 6-quart (6-L) recipes.

Please note that Instant Pot® is the registered trademark of Double Insight Inc., and that Instant Pot was designed in Canada, with healthy living, green living and ethnic diversity in mind.

DOS AND DON'TS

- Always read your manual: there are important updated details about your model of Instant Pot in there. You can always get a copy online at InstantPot.com (http://instantpot.com/benefits/specifications-and-manuals).

- Never leave any appliance alone the first time you cook in it! Why? It could be defective and cause problems. After your first test run, you can take the dog for a walk, read or generally ignore it while it's cooking your dinner.

- Never cook with a dry pressure cooker—it needs liquid to come up to pressure. Also note that if you cook something a second time using a steaming method you will probably have to add more water in the bottom before you recook it.

- Never overfill the pot. Use your thinking cap when cooking large portions of beans or grains. Remember that they will expand up to twice their size while cooking.

- Remember that cooking times are not written in stone and one bag of dried pinto beans may take a couple of minutes longer to cook than another. You can always put the lid back on and cook longer.

- Never attempt to force the lid open on your pressure cooker. If it won't open, that means the pressure has not released. It's very dangerous to force the lid!

- Never try to pressure can in your cooker; the temperature of the pressure does not get high enough to safely can. Instead, you'll need to buy a stove-top canning pressure cooker.

- Make sure the outside of the stainless steel pot is completely dry before you put it in the base.

- Double-check that the insert is in the cooker before you pour in ingredients. I always push the base under my cabinets as a signal that it needs the insert. When I pull it out I see inside, so I won't be tempted to pour water in without looking first.

- Always wash the lid well after cooking and empty the plastic condensation collector that is on the top back of the pressure cooker.

- If you live at a high elevation you will need to increase your cooking time for all recipes by a few minutes.

- Always check the pressure release valve to make sure it's clear before using each time.

- Never immerse the cord or the outside bottom of the Instant Pot in water. Clean with a damp cloth if needed.

- Remember, the outside will get hot, so keep it out of the reach of children and pets. Also keep plastics and other things that could melt away from the base.

- Do not store on your stove—there are many horror stories of melting Instant Pots and ruined stove burners.

- After cleaning, always store the stainless steel liner in the base. That way you will never accidentally pour ingredients directly into the base.

BEFORE COOKING IN YOUR INSTANT POT

1. Make sure that the area around the pot is clear. The outside will get hot and could melt plastic.

2. With that in mind, check to make sure nothing is over the steam release handle area, such as your upper cabinets. Over time the steam can damage and warp them!

3. Check the steam release valve to make sure it's clear.

4. Check that the stainless steel inner pot is in before adding ingredients.

5. Be sure to twist the lid on tight and turn the steam release valve to seal if using one of the pressure-cooking functions.

WAYS TO RELEASE THE PRESSURE

When you are using a pressure cooker, pressure builds up, and that's the reason food cooks faster than with other methods. Most important, that pressure has to get released before you can get to your dinner.

Remember that you are dealing with piping hot food no matter which method you use, so always use caution!

NATURAL PRESSURE RELEASE (NPR)

This is when you let the pressure release on its own without doing anything. Once the cooking time is done, it will switch to the warming setting automatically. Once the silver pin lowers, the pressure is released and you can open the lid.

QUICK PRESSURE RELEASE (QPR)

You will carefully turn the release valve to manually release the pressure for this one. Pay attention so that no hot liquid gets sprayed on you. I use a silicone pot holder when I use this method. You should not use this method on soup or anything with a lot of liquid because you may burn yourself once hot liquid starts shooting out of the valve. You can try opening the valve in very short bursts with a minute or two in between if you are in a hurry.

10-MINUTE RELEASE

Wait until the cook cycle has completed, then wait until the keep warm cycle counts up to 10 minutes. It's safer to move the pressure valve and you may get to eat a few minutes sooner. Warning: If it's a dish with lots of cooking liquid left, you may still have to move the pressure valve for short bursts first. Warning 2: Recipes that use natural pressure release are also using that time for extra cooking. If you open it sooner it may not be quite done.

Steam release valve

Inner stainless steel pot

The outside

CARING FOR YOUR INSTANT POT

SILICONE SEALING RING

The white gasket—or silicone sealing ring, as it's called in your manual—that seals your Instant Pot will need to be replaced about every year. If the pot is having trouble getting up to pressure on recipes it has done fine on in the past, it may be a sign to replace it. If it has any cracks or splits it must be replaced immediately.

You will probably want to have an extra one on hand. It also absorbs strong smells, and having a spare can keep your yogurt from smelling like curry. You can remove these sealing rings from the lid, so you can wash and dry it thoroughly to help keep it odor-free. You can wash this by hand or in the dishwasher. Also, storing the lid ring side up will help odors dissipate. Some people recommend taking it out and letting it sit in the sun for a day to remove odors.

STEAM RELEASE VALVE

This is on the top of the lid and is what you move to seal or to release steam. It will pop off, and you can wash it and check to make sure nothing is blocking it.

ANTI-BLOCK SHIELD

This little stainless steel "cage" protects the Instant Pot from clogging. It also comes off to be cleaned as well.

CONDENSATION COLLECTOR

This little plastic condensation collector is on the upper back of the Instant Pot base. It's made of plastic and can be removed for dumping and cleaning. It mainly collects runoff when you place the lid in the side-lid holder on the top of the base.

INNER STAINLESS STEEL POT

This can be washed by hand or even in the dishwasher. I find that if you have stuck-on or burnt food on the bottom, soaking overnight with water and dishwashing liquid will make it much easier to clean.

THE OUTSIDE

Never immerse the outside pot in water because that's where its electrical components are housed. Unplug the unit and clean with a damp cloth, then dry immediately.

WHAT DO THE RED DISPLAYS MEAN?

OFF is pretty self-explanatory. Once plugged in, the Instant Pot starts communicating with you to let you know that it's not on.

ON is also obvious, but it's nice to know that it's working!

Lid means that the lid is not on correctly and is not sealed.

Hot appears when you are using the sauté function and it has reached the set temperature.

A number like 30 is the cooking time for a pressure cooker function.

A number like 8:25 is the countdown of the delay timer.

A number that starts with L, such as L 0:45, is telling you how long the keep warm function has been running.

A number like 4:30 is the cooking time for the slow cooker function.

See your Instant Pot manual for more codes.

WHAT DO ALL THOSE BUTTONS DO?

I've heard a lot of people talk about wanting to use more of the buttons on their Instant Pots. Most of the recipes you'll find use the manual button, so you may feel like you're leaving some of that fancy functionality on the table.

All the buttons except the sauté, yogurt and slow cooker settings are actually pressure cooker shortcuts. Even steam is a special version of a pressure cooker setting. I'll explain in more detail below, but each button has a preset time and cooking level that you can still adjust manually if you like.

MOST USED BUTTONS

Keep Warm/Cancel

Press to cancel current program/cooking selection.
Adjust temperature with the adjust button (less/normal/more).

By default, the Instant Pot will keep your food warm after the cooking time has elapsed. Time will count up so that you know how long it's been on the keep-warm cycle. When you press the button it will turn the heat off.

You will use the Keep Warm/Cancel button often to end the sauté function before you start your next cooking program, such as pressure cooking added ingredients.

Sauté

Adjust temperature with the adjust button (less/normal/more).
No lid is used with this function.

This button is used to sauté right in the pot so you don't have extra cleanup. We will use it to cook onions and the like before adding the ingredients that will be finished on the manual or slow cooker settings.

The sauté function can also be used before a pressure cooking cycle to heat the pot so it will come up to pressure more quickly. Plus, you can always use it after a pressure cooking cycle if you want to reduce the amount of liquid left in the pot before serving.

Manual

Adjust cook time in minutes with the + and – buttons.
Adjust temperature with the adjust button (low/high).
Pressure cooking lid is used with this pressure cooking function and the steam release handle will be set to sealing, or closed.

This is the function you will probably find yourself using the most often.

Timer

You must select a cooking method, like manual, before you can set the time.
Adjust cook time in minutes with the + and – buttons

The timer will count down until it's time to begin cooking. This is a great function to use to make fresh steel-cut oats in the morning. You can have it set to start cooking when you wake up in the morning.

Warning: Do not put perishable food in the pot without heat for long period of times. This is best for doing a plain water and grain mixture if it will be in the pot overnight.

SPECIAL COOKING METHODS

Slow Cooker

Adjust cook time in minutes with the + and − buttons.

Adjust temperature with the adjust button (less/normal/more).

Pressure cooking lid can be used with this function and the steam release handle will be set to venting, or open, or you can purchase the Instant Pot glass lid and use that.

You may need to adjust your favorite recipes when you start cooking them in your Instant Pot. It tends to cook a little hotter, and you will get less evaporation when you use the pressure cooking lid, even with the valve open.

Steam

Defaults to 10 minutes on high pressure.

Pressing the adjust button changes the time (15 or 3 minutes).

Pressing the + and − buttons will still add and subtract minutes from the time.

This setting is unique in that it heats at full power the entire cycle. Because of this you always want to use the rack that came with your Instant Pot or a steamer insert when using this setting. It's great for dumplings and steaming vegetables.

Warning: Do not put food directly on the bottom of the pot when using the steam function—always use a steamer basket of some kind.

Rice

Defaults to low pressure.

This setting is actually fully automatic like a rice cooker, and it will adjust the cooking time depending on how much water and rice you use. That said, it's really for white rice. You'll use the manual or multigrain settings for brown and more exotic types of rice.

Yogurt

Defaults to 8 hours.

Pressing the adjust button makes big changes on this setting! It will cycle to boil, a setting to pasteurize homemade nondairy milk before you make yogurt or to 24 hours.

Pressure cooking lid can be used with this function, and the steam release handle can be open or closed.

Pressing the + and − buttons will still add and subtract hours from the time.

This just keeps the pot warm enough to allow the culture to multiply. I also use the yogurt default setting for uttapam and dosa batter.

You can make yogurt directly in the stainless steel pot or in small mason jars. I typically use some glass jars from a yogurt maker I used to have.

GENERAL PRESETS

All of these use the pressure cooking lid with the valve closed.

Soup

Defaults to 30 minutes on high pressure.
Pressing the adjust button changes the time (40 or 20 minutes).

Meat/Stew

Defaults to 35 minutes on high pressure.
Pressing the adjust button changes the time (45 or 20 minutes).

Bean/Chili

Defaults to 30 minutes on high pressure.
Pressing the adjust button changes the time (40 or 25 minutes).

Poultry

Defaults to 15 minutes on high pressure.
Pressing the adjust button changes the time (30 or 5 minutes).

Multigrain

Defaults to 40 minutes on high pressure.
Pressing the adjust button changes the time (45 or 60 minutes).

Notice that on this setting and only on the 60-minute cycle, the grain first gets a 45-minute warm water soaking time before the 60 minutes of pressure cooking time. This works great with Kamut, oat groats, wheat berries and other grains that you typically soak before cooking. Try 1 cup (190 g) unsoaked grain to 3 cups (700 ml) water or broth and cook on this setting.

Porridge or Congee

Defaults to 20 minutes on high pressure.
Pressing the adjust button changes the time (30 or 15 minutes).

TROUBLESHOOTING

If you live at a high altitude, above sea level, you will find that you need to up the cooking times by 1–5 minutes, or by about 5 percent. Once you've made a recipe the way you want it, make a note in the book, so you can make it perfectly at your altitude every time.

If your cooker isn't coming up to pressure, meaning the silver pin is not coming up, there are a few basic things to look into first.

• Check to see if the pressure valve is in the closed position.

• Twist the lid to make sure it's on tight. Sometimes if you press down a little when doing this, it will give it a boost to get to pressure.

• Did you remember to add water? Even if you are cooking on top of a rack, you will add at least 1½ cups (360 ml) water.

• Try adding additional liquid. Perhaps your recipe is too thick?

• Remember, the closer to the fill line your food is, the longer it will take to come up to pressure.

NINJA INSTANT POT TRICKS

Never enough time? Try turning on the sauté function before adding the food you plan on pressure cooking. It will help the pot come up to pressure faster, because the pot will already be hot.

In the same vein, if you are steaming something or adding plain water to your Instant Pot to begin with, add already boiling water from your kettle to kick-start the pressure building. The heat always speeds it up a little.

Cut up everything to the same size so everything cooks evenly. The ninja part comes in when you match the size of cut veggies with the cooking time. Cut quick-cooking vegetables larger and slow-cooking vegetables smaller.

Stack food in foil, foil-covered Pyrex dishes or stainless steel stackable pans to cook multiple dishes at once that will all be done at the same time! See more about this in the layered meals chapter on page 173.

Hate soaking grains as much as I do? There is a magic setting on the Instant Pot that soaks for 45 minutes and pressure cooks for 60 minutes. It's part of the multigrain button program that defaults to 40 minutes on high pressure. However, if you press the adjust button once it will look like it's going to cook for a normal 60 minutes. But on this setting—only on the multigrain 60-minute cycle—the grain first gets a 45-minute warm water soaking time before the 60 minutes pressure cooking time. It's great for Kamut and other long-cooking grains.

Barbara, of PressureCookingToday.com, had a brilliant idea to cut a silicone pastry mat to use as a sling under bowls or pans you place inside the pressure cooker. You can also do this with aluminum foil, but with the silicone you will make it once and use it forever! You can see her post about this at www.pressurecookingtoday.com/how-to-get-a-pan-out-of-the-pressure-cooker.

SPECIAL DIET CONSIDERATIONS

If you have any of my other cookbooks, or read my blog HealthySlowCooking.com, you know that I do my best to provide options in my recipes so everyone can enjoy them.

LOW OR NO SALT

In most of the recipes I ask that you add salt to taste. The recipes that do call for a certain amount is because they usually need extra seasoning or the salt needs to be added before the end. You can always substitute your favorite salt-free herb blend, or just up the seasonings in those recipes until they make you happy.

NO ADDED OIL

If you are on a no-oil diet, you will be able to make all of the recipes with a few adjustments. While I offer the option to use a small amount of oil to sauté with, you can easily dry sauté or add a little water/vegetable broth in the Instant Pot. If you find your onions or garlic sticking, just add a bit of water or vegetable broth.

Use applesauce or pumpkin puree in place of oil in the "baked" goods and use the pumpkin tamale batter to fill in place of the coconut oil tamale batter. There's always a substitute you can use. You can even replace full-fat coconut milk with low-fat or use coconut extract and plain, unsweetened nondairy milk.

GLUTEN-FREE

If you are gluten-free due to celiac disease or allergies, ALWAYS check labels on grains, sauces and the like for a clear label that says gluten-free. Remember that some grains, like oats, are often contaminated with wheat products, but there are places like Bob's Red Mill that have dedicated allergy-free facilities.

You can replace a gluten-free baking mix for whole wheat pastry flour, spelt flour and more. This is what I do in my own kitchen when I bake gluten-free.

You can replace gluten-containing grains with a gluten-free grain of a similar cooking time:

*   Wheat berries with oat groats
*   Spelt with oat groats
*   Bulgur with brown rice couscous, quinoa or millet

SOY-FREE

I've tried to provide substitutes or alternatives to soy products when used. You can use hemp tofu in many of the recipes in place of soy tofu or tempeh, and use almond or coconut milk or yogurt. You can substitute seitan, jackfruit and even chickpeas in many recipes that do call for tofu or tempeh.

NUTRITIONAL INFORMATION DISCLAIMER

Nutritional information is included in this book to give a ballpark idea on calories and the like. All of the recipes offer many options that could change the numbers drastically. If you have a medical condition that requires you to keep close track of those numbers, please enter the exact amount and ingredients that you are using into your doctor's recommended nutritional tracker.

CHAPTER 1

Five Recipes to Start You Out

If you've just unpacked your Instant Pot or have been using it for years, these are the recipes that you should make first.

One of my testers told me that The Best Not-Refried Black Beans recipe (page 24) was worth the price of the book, so it's first on my list. You'll find yourself making these all the time, and you can make an organic batch of these that are enough for dinner and some to freeze for less than the cost of one can!

I've also got a great breakfast for you—Pear Cardamom Steel-Cut Oats for Two (page 27)—as well as Thick and Rich Jackfruit Ragu (page 28), Super Easy Weeknight One-Pot Pasta (page 31) and Zucchini Lemon Spelt Snack Cake (page 32), in which you can substitute carrots during the winter. Enjoy!

THE BEST NOT-REFRIED BLACK BEANS

gluten-free, soy-free, no added oil option*

Refried beans are so inexpensive to make at home, and they can be made in less than an hour from unsoaked dried beans using the pressure cooker settings on your Instant Pot. These have no added oil and you can freeze the leftovers in burritos for grab-and-go lunches.

MAKES 14 SERVINGS

SAUTÉ INGREDIENTS

1 tbsp (15 ml) mild oil (or *dry sauté or add a little water/vegetable broth)

1½ cups (372 g) minced onion

1½ cups (225 g) minced bell pepper

4 cloves garlic, minced

1½ tsp (3 g) cumin powder

PRESSURE COOKER INGREDIENTS

3 cups (700 ml) water

2 cups (400 g) dried black beans (1 lb [453 g])

2 tsp (4 g) oregano

1½ tsp (3 g) chili powder

1 tsp jalapeño powder (page 56), optional

½ tsp chipotle powder, optional

½ tsp liquid smoke, optional

Salt, to taste

For the sauté ingredients, use the sauté setting over normal, or medium heat, and heat the oil or broth. Sauté the onion until transparent, 5 minutes. Then add the bell pepper, garlic and cumin powder and sauté until the bell peppers soften, a few minutes more.

For the pressure cooker, add the water, black beans, oregano, chili powder, and jalapeño powder, chipotle powder and/or liquid smoke (if using) to the onion mixture and stir to combine. Put the lid on, make sure the steam release handle is closed, change to the manual setting (the pressure cooking one) and set the timer for 40 minutes.

Allow the pressure to release naturally. You'll know when it's ready because the round silver pressure gauge will drop down.

Mash the beans with a potato masher or the back of a large spoon. You can leave them as chunky as you like or you can even use an immersion blender to make them completely smooth. Add salt to taste before serving.

PER ½-CUP (120-G) SERVING: Calories 52.9, protein 2.6 g, total fat 1.2 g, carbohydrates 8.6 g, sodium 1.2 mg, fiber 2.6 g

This recipe makes a lot of beans. I suggest that you freeze the extras in batches that would feed your household for one meal. Another way to save the leftovers for another time is to make burritos with them. I roll some of the beans with salsa in flour tortillas and then freeze in freezer bags or freezer-safe containers.

PEAR CARDAMOM STEEL-CUT OATS FOR TWO

gluten-free*, soy-free, no added oil

You may be surprised that you can make a small batch of oatmeal for two in your large Instant Pot. This version is full of sweet pears, cardamom and almonds. If you love the chewy texture of steel-cut oats, then you'll love the way they cook up in your Instant Pot.

MAKES 2 SERVINGS

1½ cups (355 ml) water

½ cup (40 g) steel-cut oats (*make sure oats are clearly marked gluten-free)

1 small pear, chopped (a heaping ½ cup [75 g])

⅛ tsp cardamom (a large pinch) or 1 whole green cardamom pod

2 tbsp (11.5 g) toasted sliced almonds

Sweetener of choice, to taste (optional)

Nondairy milk, for serving

Add the water, oats, pear and cardamom to your Instant Pot. Put the lid on and make sure the steam release handle is set to sealing, or closed. Select the manual setting and set to cook for 3 minutes. The Instant Pot timer will begin counting down the time once it gets up to pressure.

Allow the pressure to release naturally. You'll know when it's ready because the round silver pressure gauge will drop down.

Open, and remove the cardamom pod (if using). Serve topped with almonds, the sweetener (if using) and a drizzle of nondairy milk. If the pears are very ripe you can skip the extra sweetener.

PER SERVING: Calories 213.7, protein 8.2 g, total fat 6.1 g, carbohydrates 36.8 g, sodium 0.0 mg, fiber 6.8 g

One of my favorite features of the Instant Pot is its delay timer. Add the water, oats and cardamom and set the timer to start cooking about 20 minutes before you leave the house. That will leave you enough time to scoop it into your portable food containers and dash out to work.

THICK AND RICH JACKFRUIT RAGU

gluten-free, soy-free, no added oil option*

Sometimes you need a hearty dinner that is full of flavor and includes pasta to make everyone happy.
This thick, tomato-based sauce has carrots, celery and lots of shredded jackfruit to fill you up.

MAKES 6 SERVINGS

1–2 tbsp (15–30 ml) oil (or *dry sauté or add a little water/vegetable broth)

1 small onion, minced

4 cloves garlic, minced

2 small carrots, chopped small

1 medium stalk celery, chopped small

1 (20-oz [565-g]) can jackfruit in brine (do not use the kind in syrup)

1 (28-oz [794-g]) can tomato puree (or 3 cups [750 ml] homemade)

2 tbsp (33 g) tomato paste

1 tbsp (15 ml) balsamic vinegar

2 tsp (2 g) dried oregano

1 tsp dried basil

1 bay leaf

½ tsp salt

¼ tsp dried rosemary

¼ tsp ground black pepper

Use the sauté setting over normal, or medium heat, and heat the oil if using. Sauté the onion until transparent, 5 minutes. Then add the garlic, carrots and celery and sauté for 4 minutes more.

Rinse the jackfruit in a strainer and then smash it in your hands to get it to break into shreds. You can remove any large seedpods and discard. They will be obvious once you start smashing.

Add the jackfruit shreds, tomato puree, tomato paste, balsamic vinegar, oregano, basil, bay leaf, salt, rosemary and black pepper. Put the lid on and make sure the steam release handle is set to sealing, or closed; change to the manual setting (the pressure cooking one) and set the timer for 10 minutes.

Allow the pressure to release naturally. You'll know when it's ready because the round silver pressure gauge will drop down.

Before serving, taste and add extra salt, pepper, herbs and balsamic vinegar if needed. Remove and discard the bay leaf. Serve over toasted bread, pasta or polenta.

PER SERVING: Calories 132.9, protein 3.6 g, total fat 5.0 g, carbohydrates 21.5 g, sodium 1207.8 mg, fiber 5.6 g

Note: The nutritional information includes all the sodium that's in the jackfruit can—even the brine that you pour down the sink. This means you are ingesting less salt than is labeled.

If you can't find jackfruit where you live, try substituting shredded sweet potato or butternut squash in its place.

SUPER EASY WEEKNIGHT ONE-POT PASTA

gluten-free, soy-free, no added oil

Imagine a long day at work, you're hungry, or maybe it's unbearably hot outside. Come home, throw some pasta sauce, water and pasta into your Instant Pot, and poof—instant dinner in a cool kitchen. This recipe has been tested with whole wheat, brown rice and brown rice–quinoa pastas. It does not work well with bean pastas.

MAKES 4 SERVINGS

4 cups (980 g) pasta sauce, homemade (page 28) or store-bought

3 cups (700 ml) water

4 cups (384 g) dried, uncooked gluten-free pasta (see headnote; use spirals or penne, NOT spaghetti or tiny pasta that could clog the pressure valve)

Mix the sauce and water in the Instant Pot liner. Stir in the pasta and press under the sauce.

Click the manual button, and then click the pressure button to turn the pressure to low. Cook on low for 5 minutes.

Carefully move the pressure valve to manually release the pressure.

PER SERVING: Calories 560.0, protein 20.0 g, total fat 7.0 g, carbohydrates 104.0 g, sodium 940.0 mg, fiber 16.0 g

Jazz it up by sautéing your favorite long-cooking vegetables such as onions, bell peppers, carrots and the like right in the pot before you add the sauce and pasta. If you want to add quick-cooking ones like peas, asparagus or greens, add them after the pressure cooking. Just switch to the sauté function and let it heat until the veggies are ready to eat.

ZUCCHINI LEMON SPELT SNACK CAKE

gluten-free option*, soy-free, no added oil option**

In the summer, you have more zucchini than you know what to do with. Here's a great way to use some of it up and you don't even have to turn on the oven or get the house all heated up.

MAKES 8 SERVINGS

DRY INGREDIENTS

1¼ cups (150 g) spelt flour (or use whole wheat pastry flour or *gluten-free baking blend)

¾ tsp baking soda

¼ tsp salt

WET INGREDIENTS

2 tbsp (14 g) ground flaxseed mixed with 4 tbsp (60 ml) warm water

2 tbsp (30 ml) oil (or **use applesauce)

1 cup (124 g) shredded zucchini (about 1 small)

½ cup (100 g) raw or coconut sugar

1 tbsp (4 g) lemon zest (optional)

1 tsp lemon extract or ½ tsp lemon oil

OPTIONAL DECADENT LEMON COCONUT ICING

½ cup (109 g) coconut oil

¾ cup (90 g) powdered sugar

2 tbsp (30 ml) lemon juice

For the dry ingredients, combine the flour, baking soda and salt in a small mixing bowl, then set aside.

For the wet ingredients, combine the flaxseed mixture, oil, zucchini, sugar, lemon zest (if using) and lemon extract in a large mixing bowl. Add the dry mix to the wet one and stir well.

Oil a springform pan that fits into your Instant Pot; it will be 8 inches (20 cm) or smaller. Be sure to try to fit the pan in your Instant Pot on the rack BEFORE you pour in the batter.

Pour in the batter and spread evenly. Cover with foil. Add the rack to your Instant Pot and add 1½ cups (355 ml) water.

If your pan does not fit inside the rack handles, you will need to fashion some handles out of aluminum foil to lower the pan into the cooker. Tear off two pieces of foil about 3 feet (1 m) long, fold each one lengthwise two times. Lay the foil handles out on the counter in a plus sign near your cooker. Place your pan in the center, where the two pieces cross. Pull the handles up and carefully lift the pan into your Instant Pot.

Place the lid on with the steam release handle closed and cook on high pressure for 35 minutes.

Let the pressure release naturally. Once the pressure indicator goes down, remove the lid, lift out the pan using the foil handles and remove the foil that's covering the pan. Let cool before icing or serving.

To make the icing, add all the ingredients to a mixer fitted with the whisk attachment. Whisk until creamy and combined. Stop to scrape down the bowl several times.

Note: If you make this in the winter you will need to soften up the coconut oil first because it will be hard as a rock!

PER SERVING (FOR THE CAKE): Calories 126.0, protein 2.2 g, total fat 5.0 g, carbohydrates 22.2 g, sodium 209.7 mg, fiber 2.3 g

PER SERVING (FOR THE ICING): Calories 174.6, protein 0.0 g, total fat 14.0 g, carbohydrates 11.5 g, sodium 0.9 mg, fiber 0.0 g

CHAPTER 2

Quick and Easy Homemade Staples to Save You Money

Making my own staples is one of my favorite parts about cooking whole foods at home. I think you'll love it too once you try it. It's wonderful to know exactly what's in your food, and all your spice blends will have your favorite flavors in them.

If you have the 7-in-1 Instant Pot you will find a yogurt setting and will enjoy creating your own vegan yogurt, but not all models have it. You don't have to have an Instant Pot to make yogurt, but it does make it easy.

I have an array of no-salt-added spice blends for you to use and a recipe to make your own jalapeño powder. I've fallen in love with the bold flavor it gives beans and Mexican dishes. Plus you can use them in the other recipes in this book.

NO-EFFORT SOY YOGURT

gluten-free, no added oil

For this particular yogurt you'll want to use a fresh unopened container of store-bought soy milk. That way you know it's already pasteurized and you get to skip the step of boiling it and waiting for it to cool. Use a soy milk with as few ingredients as possible, hopefully just soybeans and water. If it has too many ingredients, it will not thicken up as much.

MAKES 4 CUPS (960 G)

1 (32-oz [946-ml]) container plain unsweetened soy milk that has soybeans and water as its only ingredients

1 packet vegan yogurt starter (I use Cultures for Health Vegan Yogurt Starter)

1 tbsp (8 g) tapioca starch (optional) as thickener

Whisk together the soy milk, starter and starch (if using) in a very clean mixing bowl. Either pour the mixture directly into the Instant Pot or pour into small glass jars. If you use glass jars you can sit them right on the pot bottom; there's no need to use a rack.

Put on the lid. You don't have to close the valve, but if you do it could help the temperature stay more consistent. Select the yogurt setting. The default time is 8 hours, but I find the yogurt gets firmer without an added thickener if you let it culture for 12 or more hours. Be aware that the yogurt will also become tangier the longer it cultures.

Store in the fridge for up to 10 days.

PER 1-CUP (240-G) SERVING: Calories 88.8, protein 7.0 g, total fat 4.0 g, carbohydrates 6.3 g, sodium 85.0 mg, fiber 1.0 g

DIY VEGAN RICOTTA

This is a down and dirty quick vegan ricotta that you can use in pasta dishes, in sandwiches or however else you want. Use it on page 171 for a delicious pasta casserole.

MAKES 3 CUPS (700 G)

1 cup (237 ml) water

1 cup (137 g) cashews, soaked in water for 6 hours, drained

¾ cup (109 g) blanched slivered almonds, soaked in water for 6 hours, drained

1–2 tbsp (5–10 g) nutritional yeast

2 tsp (10 ml) lemon juice

1 tsp apple cider vinegar

½–1 tsp salt, to taste

Add everything to your food processor or blender and process until fairly smooth, but not as smooth as plain nut butter. That way it will be closer to the texture of real ricotta.

PER ½-CUP (120-G) SERVING: Calories 241.7, protein 8.4 g, total fat 19.7 g, carbohydrates 12.1 g, sodium 3.7 mg, fiber 3.0 g

CAULIFLOWER SOUR CREAM

gluten-free, soy-free, no added oil

Since cauliflower is magic, I thought why not try making a sour cream with it? It's not an exact match, but it's pretty amazing for an oil-free version. Add more lemon juice if you'd like more bite. The cashews will make it extra smooth and creamy, but you can leave them out if you are on a nut-free diet.

MAKES ABOUT 1 CUP (240 G)

PRESSURE COOKER INGREDIENTS

2 cups (214 g) cauliflower florets

2 cups (475 ml) water

3 tbsp (26 g) cashews (optional)

BLENDER INGREDIENTS

1 tsp nutritional yeast

1 tsp lemon juice

½ tsp apple cider vinegar

2–6 tsp (10–30 ml) cooking liquid, as needed

Salt, to taste

For the pressure cooker, add the cauliflower, water and cashews (if using) to your Instant Pot and cook on high pressure for 3 minutes.

Let the pressure release naturally.

Drain, reserving the liquid for blending.

For the blender, add the cauliflower and cashews along with the nutritional yeast, lemon juice, apple cider vinegar and 1 teaspoon of the cooking liquid. Blend, scrape down the sides and add more cooking liquid if needed. Blend until smooth. Add salt to taste.

PER ¼-CUP (60-ML) SERVING: Calories 53.1, protein 2.5 g, total fat 3.1 g, carbohydrates 5.1 g, sodium 15.8 mg, fiber 1.6 g

Try this as a topping for the pierogies on page 185 or on tacos, chili and more.

NOT-RAW ALMOND MILK

gluten-free, soy-free, no added oil

Sometimes you need some nondairy milk and you don't have time to wait for your nuts to soak. This is a quick and easy way that will give you a quart (946 ml) of nondairy milk in less time than it takes to go to the store. You can use it plain for cooking or flavor it up and drink it as dessert. Please note that there are no nutritionals for this recipe because it really depends on your blending and straining. If you use a nut milk bag it should be close in calories to store-bought almond milk.

MAKES 4 CUPS (946 ML)

PRESSURE COOKER INGREDIENTS

2 cups (475 ml) water

1 cup (145 g) almonds

BLENDER INGREDIENTS

4 cups (946 ml) water

Extras from the list below

EXTRAS

2 tsp (10 ml) pure vanilla extract

3 tbsp (36 g) melted vegan chocolate chips, for chocolate milk

½ cup (75 g) strawberries, blueberries or other berry

1 tsp ground chia seeds, to thicken

Sweetener of choice, to taste

For the pressure cooker, add the water and almonds to your Instant Pot and cook on high pressure for 10 minutes.

Let the pressure release naturally.

Drain the almonds. I like to slip them out of their skins and discard for smoother milk, but you can leave them on if you prefer.

For the blender, add the almonds and the 4 cups (946 ml) water to your blender and blend well. Strain through a nut milk bag and store in the refrigerator.

The recipe makes an unsweetened plain nondairy milk that many of the recipes in this book call for. But there's no need to stop there. You can add one or more of the extras to the blender with the strained milk and blend again.

INSTANT POT VEGETABLE BOUILLON

I always like to have homemade bouillon on hand. It's ridiculously cheap to make and you can freeze it, too. I freeze mine in ice-cube trays that are about 2 tablespoons (30 ml) per cube. Once frozen, pop out and store in a resealable bag in the freezer. Use as you would a normal bouillon cube in recipes.

MAKES ABOUT 4 CUPS (940 G)

PRESSURE COOKER INGREDIENTS

½ cup (120 ml) water

2 large onions, quartered

6 medium carrots, cut into lengths to fit Instant Pot

4 celery stalks, cut into lengths to fit Instant Pot

8 (3" [7.5-cm]) sprigs fresh thyme or 3 tsp (3 g) dried thyme

1 (3" [7.5-cm]) sprig fresh rosemary or 1 tsp dried rosemary

BLENDER INGREDIENTS

1 cup (96 g) nutritional yeast

Salt, to taste (optional)

For the pressure cooker, add the water, onions, carrots, celery and herbs to your Instant Pot and put the lid on. Cook on manual with high pressure for 10 minutes.

Let the pressure release naturally.

For the blender, carefully scoop the cooked veggies and broth into your blender and add the nutritional yeast. Blend until smooth. Add salt (if using) and blend again.

Store what you can use in a week in the refrigerator. Put the rest in ice-cube trays and freeze.

PER 2-TABLESPOON (30-G) SERVING: Calories 21.4, protein 2.1 g, total fat 0.0 g, carbohydrates 3.4 g, sodium 15.1 mg, fiber 1.2 g

HOMEMADE MUSHROOM STOCK

gluten-free, soy-free, no added oil

Sometimes you need a broth that's full of natural umami. I love adding nutritional yeast to create that effect, but it doesn't go with everything. This mushroom broth is a great sub for beef broth to veganize old favorites like French onion soup. It's great in Becky's congee on page 152 and with the Mix and Match Miso Soup on page 151.

MAKES 8 CUPS (1.9 L)

8 cups (1893 ml) water

4 cups (280 g) sliced white mushrooms (about ½ lb [225 g])

2 cups (230 g) sliced onion or leeks

½ cup assorted dried mushrooms (different kinds of dried mushrooms weigh vastly different amounts—please measure by volume)

1 tsp salt (optional)

1 tsp minced garlic

15 whole black peppercorns

Put all the ingredients into your Instant Pot. Put the lid on and make sure the pressure valve is closed. Cook on high pressure for 8 minutes.

Allow the pressure to release naturally.

Strain out all the solids and store the stock in the fridge for 5–7 days, or freeze in ice-cube trays to use another time.

PER ½-CUP (120-ML) SERVING: Calories 11.2, protein 0.8 g, total fat 0.1 g, carbohydrates 2.3 g, sodium 1.1 mg, fiber 0.5 g

You could make this just with dried mushrooms if that's all you have on hand. Just up the amount to 1 cup.

PLAIN APPLESAUCE WITH VARIATIONS

gluten-free, soy-free, no added oil

I use applesauce in oatmeal, to replace the oil in baking and even as a topping or sauce. All that just from a few simple apples. It's pretty amazing, right? Plus you can make it when apples are the freshest and freeze for use all year long. Or you can be like me and use it for the apples you almost forgot you had!

MAKES ABOUT 5 CUPS (1.2 KG)

4 lb (1.8 kg) apples

1 cup (237 ml) water

Peel the apples, core them and cut into chunks. Add to your Instant Pot with the water and cook on high pressure for 10 minutes.

Let the pressure release naturally.

Drain the water, or use a slotted spoon to remove the apples from the liner and put in a food processor or blender. Blend until smooth.

Keep what you will use in the refrigerator for up to 5 days and freeze the rest in the sizes you typically use it. For me, that's ½ cup (123 g).

PER ½-CUP (123-G) SERVING: Calories 91.0, protein 0.4 g, total fat 0.3 g, carbohydrates 24.2 g, sodium 0.5 mg, fiber 4.2 g

LEMON-THYME APPLESAUCE

This really is when applesauce turns into a full-fledged sauce. Try this over baked tofu or on top of the pierogies on page 185.

MAKES ABOUT 2½ CUPS (473 G)

½ recipe Plain Applesauce (about 2½ cups [612 g])

1-2 tsp (5-10 ml) lemon juice, to taste

1 tsp fresh thyme leaves

Pinch of salt (optional)

Blend all the ingredients together in the blender.

PER ½-CUP (123-G) SERVING: Calories 91.2, protein 0.0 g, total fat 0.3 g, carbohydrates 24.2 g, sodium 0.5 mg, fiber 4.2 g

CHAI APPLESAUCE

This is the perfect topping for oatmeal or granola.

MAKES ABOUT 2½ CUPS (473 G)

½ recipe Plain Applesauce (about 2½ cups [612 g])

½ tsp ground cinnamon

¼ tsp ground cardamom

⅛ tsp ground nutmeg

1⁄16 (or large pinch) ground cloves

Blend all the ingredients together in the blender.

PER ½-CUP (123 G) SERVING: Calories 91.6, protein 0.0 g, total fat 0.3 g, carbohydrates 24.4 g, sodium 0.6 mg, fiber 4.3 g

FRESH TOMATO MARINARA SAUCE

gluten-free, soy-free, no added oil option*

I love to make my own sauces from scratch. It's cheaper than store-bought, I know where my tomatoes came from and, if I'm lucky, I can score some cheap "ugly" tomatoes. No matter what, it's always a treat to heat up some of my summer sauce in the winter.

MAKES ABOUT 4 CUPS (946 ML)

SAUTÉ INGREDIENTS

1 tbsp (15 ml) oil (or *dry sauté or add a little water/vegetable broth)

1½ cups (240 g) chopped onion

6 cloves garlic, minced

1 cup (150 g) chopped bell pepper

PRESSURE COOKER INGREDIENTS

6 cups diced fresh tomatoes (measure by volume, not weight)

2 tbsp (33 g) tomato paste

1 tbsp (16 g) balsamic vinegar

2 tsp (2 g) dried basil (or blend in 1 tbsp [4 g] fresh basil after cooking)

2 tsp (2 g) dried marjoram or oregano (or blend in 1 tbsp [4 g] fresh oregano after cooking)

1 tsp salt, or to taste

For the sauté, use the sauté setting over normal, or medium heat, and heat the oil (if using). Add the onion and sauté until transparent, 5 minutes. Then add the garlic and bell pepper and sauté for 3 minutes more.

For the pressure cooker, add the tomatoes, tomato paste, vinegar, herbs and salt to the onion mixture and stir to combine. Put the lid on and make sure that the steam release handle is set to sealing, or closed. Cook on manual setting at high pressure and set for 30 minutes.

Carefully move the pressure valve to release the pressure manually. If there's too much liquid, switch back to the sauté setting and heat until the extra liquid evaporates.

You can leave it as is, but I like to blend it with an immersion blender or in a regular blender.

Taste and season as needed. Store in the fridge for up to a week or freeze in meal-size portions in resealable plastic bags.

PER ½-CUP (120-ML) SERVING: Calories 67.7, protein 2.0 g, total fat 2.3 g, carbohydrates 11.8 g, sodium 47.0 mg, fiber 2.5 g

There are all kinds of tomatoes. While Italian paste tomatoes are the best for sauce, you can use any kind. The only difference will be that your sauce will have more liquid without paste tomatoes. The solution is to simmer it on the saute setting without a lid until it thickens.

Hate bell pepper? Leave it out, or use mushrooms instead, or some other vegetable you have in the fridge that seems to fit. Vary the herbs and even the vegetables and amounts to create your new favorite sauce. Make extra all summer long and freeze it for a treat in the middle of winter.

DIY ANDOUILLE SEITAN SAUSAGE

You can buy vegan andouille sausages, but I know some of you prefer to make all your staples from scratch and it's hard to find any that are soy-free. Andouille is a little spicy and has a Cajun flavor to it. You can use this same recipe with different spices to make other kinds of sausage links.

MAKES 8 LARGE LINKS

1½ cups (355 ml) water

1½ cups (182 g) vital wheat gluten flour

¼ cup (24 g) nutritional yeast

1 tsp dried thyme

1 tsp dried marjoram

1 tsp garlic powder

1 tsp onion powder

1 tsp cayenne powder, or to taste

1 tsp salt

½ tsp ground black pepper

¼ tsp ground allspice

Add the water, vital wheat gluten flour, nutritional yeast, thyme, marjoram, garlic powder, onion powder, cayenne, salt, black pepper and allspice to a mixer and mix on low speed for about 5 minutes. You could also knead in a bread maker or by hand until the dough begins to smooth out.

Cut into 8 equal pieces and roll into logs. I wrap mine in parchment paper, then add all of those to a large foil packet. You can also wrap them individually in foil and put them like that straight into the Instant Pot.

Add the rack to your Instant Pot and pour in 1½ cups (355 ml) water. Place the packets on top. Cook on high pressure for 35 minutes.

Allow the pressure to release naturally.

PER SERVING (1 LINK): Calories 96.7, protein 19.0 g, total fat 0.4 g, carbohydrates 4.4 g, sodium 6.6 mg, fiber 0.8 g

Try making these with the Italian Spice Blend on page 59, or even make curried ones by using the Garam Masala Spice Blend on page 64.

TEQUILA-LIME JALAPEÑO REALLY HOT SAUCE

gluten-free, soy-free, no added oil

This is one of those cool pressure cooker tricks. It takes very little effort to make your own hot sauce, and it makes great holiday gifts in fancy jars. Just be sure you keep this stored in the fridge or freezer. You can vary this with different color peppers or liquor (or make it alcohol-free), and you can even add fruit like pineapple or mango to it.

MAKES ABOUT 3 CUPS (750 G)

PRESSURE COOKER INGREDIENTS

½ lb (225 g) fresh jalapeños, stem end cut off and thickly sliced

¾ cup (175 ml) water

2 tsp (6 g) minced garlic

2 tsp (12 g) salt

BLENDER INGREDIENTS

½ cup (120 g) apple cider vinegar or white vinegar

¼ cup (55 g) agave nectar or maple syrup

¼ cup (60 ml) tequila

2 tbsp (30 ml) lime juice

For the pressure cooker, add the jalapeños, water, garlic and salt to your Instant Pot. Put on the lid and close the pressure valve. Cook on high pressure for 2 minutes.

Let the pressure release naturally.

For the blender, you can use an immersion blender and add the vinegar, agave, tequila and lime juice to the pot or carefully pour the hot pepper mixture into your blender with the blender ingredients. Either way, blend until smooth. You can strain if you want to, but I leave it as is.

Pour into jars and store in the fridge up to 2 months. Be sure to share some with your friends.

PER 1-TABLESPOON (15-ML) SERVING: Calories 8.3, protein 0.1 g, total fat 0.0 g, carbohydrates 1.8 g, sodium 0.1 mg, fiber 0.1 g

If you are not a fan of really hot sauces, you can either buy mild jalapeños or remove the seeds before cooking.

MAKE YOUR OWN JALAPEÑO POWDER

I am in love with jalapeño powder. It adds a burst of unique flavor to beans, chili and so much more. Some of my testers were having trouble finding it so I created this easy recipe for you to make your own. Use it on many dishes in this book like the Vegan Cauliflower Queso (page 138) and Southern Style Pinto Beans (page 73).

MAKES ABOUT 3 TABLESPOONS (45 G)

6 large fresh jalapeños

Mince the flesh of the jalapeño, discarding the stems and seeds.

Spread in thin layers in your dehydrator. I use the solid inserts in mine so the peppers don't fall through. Dehydrate on the setting recommended for vegetables on your dehydrator. For my cheap round one, that's 135°F (57°C). I dehydrated mine for 24 hours.

If you don't have a dehydrator, you can use the oven. Preheat the oven to 200°F (100°C), place the minced pepper on a baking sheet covered with parchment paper and leave in the oven until dry (2–3 hours).

Put in a spice grinder or blender to make into powder. The jalapeños must be completely dried before you do this step or you won't be able to grind it into powder. It will take several minutes to grind to a powder, so don't give up too soon!

You can do this for any peppers, hot or bell, whichever ones you get your hands on. That means that you can savor all the peppers you find at the farmers' market or grow in your garden all year long. Try making some bell pepper powder to add to your favorite pasta sauces and soups.

DIY SPICE BLENDS

ITALIAN SPICE BLEND

gluten-free, soy-free, no added oil

This is a basic spice blend that I use all the time. If you don't have a large herb/spice drawer, try buying exactly the amounts you need for this recipe at your local health food store or co-op. It will be so much cheaper than buying a bottle of a premade blend. Use it in the Thick and Rich Jackfruit Ragu (page 28) or to jazz up bottled sauce in the Super Easy Weeknight One-Pot Pasta (page 31).

MAKES ABOUT ⅓ CUP (15 G)

1 tbsp (4 g) dried basil

1 tbsp (5 g) dried oregano

1 tbsp (2 g) dried marjoram

1 tbsp (4 g) dried thyme

1 tsp dried rosemary or ½ tsp ground

1 tsp dried parsley

½ tsp granulated garlic

½ tsp onion powder

Add everything to a food processor and process until uniform. Store in an airtight jar.

If you want to make an Italian sausage spice, add some red pepper flakes and fennel seeds.

CAJUN SPICE BLEND

If you're looking for a salt-free version or just can't find it in your area, this little recipe will keep you in spicy goodness for a while. The best part is you can make it as spicy or mild as you want! Use it in the Easy Andouille Jambalaya (page 156).

MAKES ABOUT 2½ TABLESPOONS (40 G)

2 tsp (4 g) paprika

2 tsp (2 g) dried thyme

2 tsp (2 g) dried oregano or marjoram

1 tsp garlic powder

½ tsp onion powder

½–1 tsp cayenne pepper (depending on heat preference)

¼ tsp black pepper

¼ tsp allspice

⅛ tsp ground cloves

You can just mix all the ingredients well and store in a lidded container. You can also use a spice grinder to make it more like store-bought and to distribute the spices more evenly.

KATHY'S NO-SALT CHILI POWDER SPICE BLEND

There used to be a chili powder blend that I was in love with. Of course, it was discontinued. This is my version that I always keep in my spice cabinet. I added in the smoked paprika just to lend the smoky flavor I love. If you don't like it, then leave it out. There are a few different kinds of chiles in this. You can find these in a Hispanic market or online, or dry the chiles and make your own like the jalapeño powder on page 56. Use this in my Mushroom and Butternut Squash Chili Bean Soup (page 148).

MAKES ABOUT ¼ CUP (30 G)

1 tbsp (6 g) ground cumin

1 tbsp (6 g) smoked paprika

1 tbsp (6 g) ground guajillo pepper

2 tsp (6 g) cocoa powder

1½ tsp (1.5 g) ground oregano

1 tsp ground ancho chile powder

1 tsp granulated garlic

1 tsp onion powder

½ tsp ground cayenne chile powder

½ tsp ground coriander

¼ tsp ground chipotle chile powder

¼ tsp ground cinnamon

Mix all the ingredients together and store in an airtight container. Use more or less of the spicy chile powders to make it just the way your family likes it.

You can get the ground dried chile peppers in bulk herb sections in your local health food store or co-op. You can buy 1 teaspoon at a time, which makes this super budget-friendly.

GARAM MASALA SPICE BLEND

gluten-free, soy-free, no added oil

There are as many variations of this foundational Indian spice blend as there are families.
Feel free to tweak this basic recipe to your tastes. Be sure to try it in all the Indian recipes!

MAKES ABOUT ¼ CUP (30 G)

¼ cup (20 g) coriander seeds

10 cardamom pods

1 tbsp (9 g) peppercorns

2 tsp (4 g) cumin seeds

1 tsp ground ginger

2 cinnamon sticks

4 whole cloves

3 bay leaves

½ tsp ground chile powder

Toast all the spices in a nonstick pan until they become fragrant, 5–10 minutes. Grind in a spice or coffee grinder. Store in an airtight container.

You can use ground spices in the mix if that's what you have in your pantry, but toast them for only a minute.

CHAPTER 3

Bean and Lentil Recipes that Cook in Half the Time

Beans and lentils are the basis of a delicious and versatile vegan diet. The Instant Pot was made for beans and cuts the cooking time. Whether you soak your beans or not, you will have dinner in half the time.

COOKING DRIED BEANS

Your budget is going to love you after you start cooking dried beans instead of buying canned ones. There's no salt or additives in dried beans, and they're cheaper, too.

You can cook up a batch of plain beans and freeze to use later. I freeze mine in 1½ cups (375 g), so they can easily replace a can of beans in a recipe.

Some of the recipes will call for soaked beans and others for those that have not been soaked. The truth is that you can cook them either way in the Instant Pot. I'm not here to tell you one way is right, because I actually do it both ways.

People who do soak beans believe that it makes them easier to digest, and they always discard the soaking water. Others believe that when you soak beans and throw out the water you are discarding flavor. You'll find both methods in different parts of the world.

For me, I soak if I'm planning ahead and I don't if it's a last-minute decision. Either way, I end up with a wonderful meal from my Instant Pot.

If you are an advocate of soaking, you can adjust the water down 1 cup (237 ml) on recipes that call for unsoaked beans. For something like the Thai Red Curry Chickpea Spread (page 85), I started from dried beans so that the dish can be made at the last minute, but it would work with soaked beans if you change the cooking time to 23 minutes.

Alternatively, if you are in the no-soaking camp you can add an extra 1 cup (237 ml) water and cook for twice as long. Be aware that some recipes call for soaking, so all of the ingredients, including the beans, will cook in the same amount of time.

BEAN AND LENTIL COOKING CHART

I think of beans in three categories: quick cooking, in-between cooking and long cooking. The thing about beans is that they defy exact cooking times.

The beans you bought yesterday might not be uber-fresh; often they are at the warehouse for a long time or even just on store shelves for a while. The older the beans are, the longer they will need to cook. Think of cooking times as a rule of thumb and remember you can always cook underdone beans more by simply putting the lid back on and setting the manual function to cook for another 5 minutes or so. However, if you overcook them, you can't go back. But luckily you can always make refried beans from mushy beans, so don't fret!

In general, for every 1 cup (200 g) of dried beans you will use 2–3 cups (470–700 ml) of water.

QUICK-COOKING BEANS/LENTILS

No soaking is required for these beans and lentils, but you can halve the time if you choose to soak them.

NAME OF BEAN	UNSOAKED BEAN TIME
Beluga Lentils	4–6 minutes
Green French Lentils	5–7 minutes
Brown Lentils	6–8 minutes
Red Lentils	4–6 minutes
Split Peas	5–8 minutes

IN-BETWEEN COOKING BEANS

These beans don't really require soaking and typically cook on the stove for 30 minutes to 1 hour.

NAME OF BEAN	SOAKED BEAN TIME	UNSOAKED BEAN TIME
Adzuki Beans	6–9 minutes	15–20 minutes
Black-Eyed Peas	3–5 minutes	15–20 minutes
Cranberry Beans	7–9 minutes	20–25 minutes
Lima Beans	7–9 minutes	20–25 minutes
Navy Beans	5–8 minutes	15–20 minutes
Pinto Beans	4–6 minutes	15–20 minutes

LONG-COOKING BEANS

These beans can take as long as 4 hours when cooked on the stove, so you are saving a ton of time whether you soak or not!

NAME OF BEAN	SOAKED BEAN TIME	UNSOAKED BEAN TIME
Cannellini Beans	9–11 minutes	22–27 minutes
Black Beans	9–11 minutes	22–27 minutes
Chickpeas	12–15 minutes	35–45 minutes
Kidney Beans	9–11 minutes	22–27 minutes
Soybeans	18–23 minutes	40–45 minutes

TOMATILLO-POBLANO WHITE BEANS

gluten-free, soy-free, no added oil

These tangy beans can be used as a side, in a burrito or on top of your favorite grain with a side of sautéed veggies. I love the bold flavor of the poblanos mixed with tangy tomatillos.

MAKES 6 SERVINGS

SAUTÉ INGREDIENTS

2 cups (264 g) chopped tomatillos

1 cup (105 g) chopped poblano (seeds and stem removed before chopping)

1 cup (160 g) chopped onion

½ jalapeño without seeds (or use more to make it hotter)

1½ tsp ground cumin

PRESSURE COOKER INGREDIENTS

1½ cups (275 g) dried Great Northern beans, soaked for 8–12 hours and drained

1½ cups (355 ml) water

2 tsp dried oregano

Salt and pepper, to taste

For the sauté, add the tomatillos, poblano, onion and jalapeño to your blender or food processor. Pulse until the veggies are in tiny pieces, but not pureed.

Use the sauté setting over normal, or medium heat, and pour in the blended veggies; add the cumin and stir to combine. Cook for about 4 minutes to remove the edge off the onions and make the cumin more fragrant.

For the pressure cooker, add the beans, water and oregano to the sauté mixture and stir to combine. Put the lid on and make sure that the steam release handle is sealed. Cook on manual setting at high pressure and set for 35 minutes.

Allow the pressure to release naturally.

If there is still more liquid in the pot than you'd like to have, switch back to the sauté setting and simmer to allow some of the liquid to evaporate.

Add salt and pepper to taste before serving.

PER SERVING: Calories 83.5, protein 4.7 g, total fat 0.7 g, carbohydrates 15.9 g, sodium 107.1 mg, fiber 4.9 g

SOUTHERN-STYLE PINTO BEANS

gluten-free, soy-free, no added oil option*

My mother had a tiny garden; it was a strip in front of our screened-in porch. In it she grew about three tomato plants, petunias and a few hot pepper plants. The tomatoes were for tomato sandwiches, but the jalapeños were to spice up her pot of pinto beans. She served hers with white bread to sop up the juices, but I recommend using the Whole-Grain Cornbread on page 109. You can even cook the two of them together in your Instant Pot by adding a rack over the beans!

MAKES 4 SERVINGS

SAUTÉ INGREDIENTS

1 tbsp (15 ml) mild oil (or *dry sauté or add a little water/vegetable broth)

1½ cups (240 g) minced onion

4 cloves garlic, minced

PRESSURE COOKER INGREDIENTS

3 cups (700 ml) water

2 cups (386 g) dried pinto beans

1 tsp jalapeño powder (page 56), optional

1 tsp liquid smoke

Salt, to taste

TOPPINGS

Chopped raw onions

Chopped fresh jalapeño pepper

Vegan bacon

Chow-chow (pickled veggies)

For the sauté, use the sauté setting over normal, or medium heat, and heat the oil or broth. Add the onion and sauté until transparent, 5 minutes. Then add the garlic and sauté a minute more.

For the pressure cooker, add the water, pinto beans, jalapeño powder and liquid smoke to the onion mixture and stir to combine. Put the lid on and make sure the steam release handle is set to sealing, *or* closed; change to the manual setting (the pressure cooking one) and set the timer for 45 minutes.

Allow the pressure to release naturally.

PER SERVING: Calories 175.4, protein 7.9 g, total fat 4.1 g, carbohydrates 28.1 g, sodium 5.8 mg, fiber 8.5 g

SUSAN VOISIN'S KIDNEY BEANS IN CURRY SAUCE

gluten-free, soy-free option*, no added oil

Many of you know Susan Voisin from her popular blog, FatFreeVegan.com. She makes wonderful recipes and is one of the nicest people I have ever met. She was kind enough to let me share her recipe for one of my favorite Indian dishes with you. The kidney beans make this hearty and the spices are what will have you craving this again and again. Serve over rice or with your favorite vegan Indian bread.

MAKES 6 SERVINGS

BEAN INGREDIENTS

2 cups (386 g) dried kidney beans, soaked for at least 8 hours and drained

6 cups (1400 ml) water

1 tbsp (6 g) grated ginger

1 tsp salt

SAUCE INGREDIENTS

1 onion, minced

1 tsp minced garlic

½ tsp ajwain seeds or dried thyme

2 cups (280 g) finely diced tomatoes

¼ cup (60 g) unsweetened nondairy yogurt, homemade (page 36) or store-bought (or *use coconut yogurt)

2 tbsp (12 g) ground coriander

1 tsp ground fenugreek

¾ tsp turmeric

1 tsp garam masala

⅛ tsp ground red chile pepper or cayenne (or to taste)

Chopped cilantro, for garnish (optional)

For the beans, rinse the soaked kidney beans and put them in your Instant Pot along with the water, ginger and the salt. Cook on high pressure for 10 minutes.

Allow the pressure to release naturally.

Carefully pour the beans into another pot or stainless steel bowl. Leave them in their cooking liquid while you make the sauce. Wash and dry the insert to make the sauce.

For the sauce, use the sauté setting over normal, or medium heat. Sauté the onion until it starts to brown, stirring constantly. Add the garlic and ajwain and stir for 1 minute.

Mix in the tomatoes and cook until their liquid has evaporated, about 5 minutes. Stir in the nondairy yogurt, coriander, fenugreek, turmeric, garam masala and chile pepper.

Drain 2 cups (470 ml) of liquid from the beans and stir half of it into the sauce. Add the beans to the sauce and mix well. If the sauce is too thick or dry, add some or all of the reserved bean cooking liquid.

Simmer over low heat on the sauté setting, stirring occasionally, for at least 20 minutes, until the sauce has thickened and the flavors have blended. Check the seasonings and add salt to taste.

Transfer to a serving dish, garnish with the cilantro (if using) and serve with basmati rice, chapatis, parathas or naan.

PER SERVING: Calories 240.0, protein 16.0 g, total fat 1.0 g, carbohydrates 44.0 g, sodium 386.0 mg, fiber 17.0 g

In a big hurry or just forgot to soak your kidney beans? Try subbing unsoaked, dried black-eyed peas and cook them for 8 minutes instead of 10. Everything else will stay the same and you will still have a delicious curry!

BLACK CHICKPEA CURRY (KALA CHANA)

gluten-free, soy-free, no added oil option*

I had this curry for the first time at a local Indian restaurant, Vimala's Curry Blossom. I loved the firm, dark chickpeas in a tomato-based curry. You can make this with regular chickpeas if you can't find the black ones, but be aware that the black ones don't soften up as much as the regular ones do.

MAKES 6 SERVINGS

SAUTÉ INGREDIENTS

1 tbsp (15 ml) mild oil (or *dry sauté or add a little water/vegetable broth)

2 cups (320 g) minced onion

3 tsp (9 g) minced garlic

2 tsp (4 g) cumin seeds

2 tsp (4 g) garam masala

½ tsp ground coriander

½ tsp ground turmeric

½ tsp ground chile

PRESSURE COOKER INGREDIENTS

1½ cups (355 ml) water

1 cup (152 g) black chickpeas (or regular), soaked at least 8 hours, drained

1½ cups (270 g) diced tomatoes

2 tbsp (12 g) grated ginger

2 tsp (1 g) crushed curry leaves (optional)

Salt, to taste

For the sauté, use the sauté setting over normal or medium heat, and heat the oil or broth. Add the onion and sauté until transparent, 5 minutes. Then add the garlic, cumin seeds, garam masala, coriander, turmeric and chile and sauté for 2 more minutes.

For the pressure cooker, add the water, chickpeas, tomatoes, ginger and curry leaves to the onion mixture and stir to combine. Put the lid on and make sure the steam release handle is closed; change to the manual setting (the pressure cooking one) and set the timer for 8 minutes.

Allow the pressure to release naturally.

Before serving, mix in salt to taste. Serve over rice or with naan.

PER SERVING: Calories 101.6, protein 3.1 g, total fat 3.0 g, carbohydrates 16.6 g, sodium 125.7 mg, fiber 3.3 g

KIDNEY BEAN ÉTOUFFÉE

gluten-free, soy-free, no added oil option*

You get great flavors in this Cajun dish from the spices. Be sure to smash some of the cooked beans to thicken up your stew. Serve over brown rice, quinoa or sorghum for a change of pace.

MAKES 4 SERVINGS

SAUTÉ INGREDIENTS

1 tbsp (15 ml) mild oil (or *dry sauté or add a little water/vegetable broth)

1 cup (160 g) minced onion

2 cups (300 g) minced bell pepper

2 tsp (6 g) minced garlic

PRESSURE COOKER INGREDIENTS

1 cup (237 ml) water

1 cup (184 g) dried kidney beans, soaked for 8-12 hours** and drained

3 bay leaves

1½ tsp (1.5 g) dried thyme

2 tsp (4 g) smoked paprika

2 tsp (2 g) dried marjoram

½ tsp ground cayenne pepper (use more if you like things spicy)

BEFORE SERVING INGREDIENTS

1 (14.5-oz [411-g]) can crushed or diced tomatoes

1 tsp dried oregano

½ tsp liquid smoke (optional)

Pinch of ground bay leaf (optional)

Salt and pepper, to taste (I used 1½ tsp [9 g] salt and ½ tsp black pepper)

SERVING INGREDIENTS

Cooked rice of your choice

Hot sauce

For the sauté, use the sauté setting over normal, or medium heat, and heat the oil or broth. Add the onion and sauté until transparent, 5 minutes. Then add the bell pepper and garlic. Sauté until the bell peppers soften, 5 minutes longer.

For the pressure cooker, add the water, beans, bay leaves, thyme, smoked paprika, marjoram and cayenne to the onion mixture and stir to combine. Put the lid on and make sure the steam release handle is set to sealing, or closed; change to the manual setting (the pressure cooking one) and set the timer for 15 minutes.

Carefully manually release the pressure. Remove the bay leaves.

Before serving, mix in the crushed tomatoes, oregano, liquid smoke and ground bay leaf (if using). Then add salt and pepper to taste. Cook the stew for an additional 3 minutes on high pressure, then release the pressure naturally.

Serve over steamed rice with a side of your favorite hot sauce. I love garlic Tabasco myself.

PER SERVING (not including rice): Calories 154.5, protein 6.2 g, total fat 4.2 g, carbohydrates 25.9 g, sodium 356.7 mg, fiber 7.6 g

**When I soak beans I always put them in a large mixing bowl and fill it as close to the top with water as I can. You can always use any left over to water plants around the house, so there's really no waste.

JILL NUSSINOW'S SMOKY SWEET BLACK-EYED PEAS AND GREENS

gluten-free, soy-free, no added oil option*

Don't just reserve black-eyed peas for New Year's luck. The combination of sweet, smoky and hot and the freshness of the greens is delicious any time of the year. This recipe is from my friend, Jill Nussinow, or as you may know her, the Veggie Queen (TheVeggieQueen.com). Be sure to check out her pressure cooker cookbook, *Vegan Under Pressure*.

MAKES 6 SERVINGS

SAUTÉ INGREDIENTS

1 tsp (5 ml) oil (or *dry sauté or add a little water/vegetable broth)

1 medium to large onion, thinly sliced

3 cloves garlic, minced

1 cup (149 g) diced red pepper

1 small jalapeño or other hot chile, minced

PRESSURE COOKER FIRST COOK

2 tsp (4 g) smoked paprika

1–2 tsp (3–5 g) chili powder

1½ cups (218 g) dried black-eyed peas, soaked overnight and drained

4 dates, finely chopped

1½ cups (355 ml) water or vegetable broth, plus more as needed

PRESSURE COOKER SECOND COOK

1 (15-oz [425-g]) can fire-roasted tomatoes with green chiles

2 cups (32 g) chopped greens (such as kale, collards or Swiss chard)

Salt to taste

FOR SERVING

Hot sauce such as Tabasco or Texas Pete

For the sauté, use the sauté setting over normal, or medium heat, and heat the oil (if using). Add the onion and sauté until transparent, 5 minutes. Then add the garlic and peppers and sauté for a minute more.

For the first pressure cook, add the smoked paprika, chili powder and black-eyed peas and stir. Add the dates and water but do not stir. Put the lid on the Instant Pot and cook at high pressure for 3 minutes. Let the pressure release naturally.

For the second pressure cook, open the lid carefully. Add the tomatoes and greens. Return to high pressure for 1 more minute, then turn the valve to release manually. Add salt to taste.

To serve, you can add as much hot sauce as you want to the pot or pass it at the table so diners can add it themselves.

PER SERVING WITH KALE: Calories 94.2, protein 3.1 g, total fat 1.2 g, carbohydrates 19.8 g, sodium 296.9 mg, fiber 4.0 g

ALL THE BEANS SOUP

gluten-free, soy-free, no added oil option*

I love beans. If writing *The Great Vegan Bean Book* didn't prove that, then this soup certainly does. Even if the bean mix you use is slightly different, there will still be a mix of creamy and hearty beans, lentils and barley all harmonized with some tasty herbs and butternut squash. It's a treat during chilly evenings or packed in a thermos for lunch.

MAKES 6 SERVINGS

SAUTÉ INGREDIENTS

1 tbsp (15 ml) mild oil (or *dry sauté or add a little water/vegetable broth)

1 cup (160 g) minced onion

½ cup (75 g) minced bell pepper

2 tsp (6 g) minced garlic

PRESSURE COOKER INGREDIENTS

7 cups (1.6 L) water

1 (16-oz [454-g]) bag mixed soup beans with barley (or add ¼ cup [45 g] pearled or hulled barley to a bag that doesn't have it already)

2 stalks celery, diced

2 cups (360 g) diced butternut squash

3 bay leaves

1 tbsp (5 g) dried thyme

1 tsp smoked paprika

BEFORE SERVING INGREDIENTS

½ tsp ground rosemary or ½ tsp regular dried

½ tsp liquid smoke (optional)

¼ cup (24 g) nutritional yeast

Salt and pepper, to taste (I used 1½ tsp [9 g] salt and ½ tsp black pepper)

For the sauté, use the sauté setting over normal, or medium heat, and heat the oil or broth. Add the onion and sauté until transparent, 5 minutes. Then add the bell pepper and garlic. Sauté until the bell peppers soften, 5 minutes.

For the pressure cooker, add the water, beans, celery, butternut squash, bay leaves, thyme and smoked paprika to the onion mixture and stir to combine. Put the lid on and make sure the steam release handle is closed; change to the manual setting (the pressure cooking one) and set the timer for 40 minutes.

Allow the pressure to release naturally. Remove and discard the bay leaves.

Before serving, mix in the ground rosemary, liquid smoke and nutritional yeast and add salt and pepper to taste. I like to serve mine with a side of chipotle salt to add a little kick to it.

PER SERVING: Calories 213.4, protein 10.1 g, total fat 3.2 g, carbohydrates 39.5 g, sodium 6.9 mg, fiber 11.6 g

If you can't find a bean soup mix in your area, use equal parts small red beans, navy or Great Northern beans, baby lima beans, black beans, pinto beans, baby garbanzo beans, black-eyed or yellow-eyed peas, green and yellow split peas, brown lentils and pearled barley. You can make a large jar of your own mix to use as needed.

THAI RED CURRY CHICKPEA SPREAD

gluten-free, soy-free, no added oil

This is one step beyond the traditional vegan hummus staple. It gets some spice from Thai red curry paste, richness from coconut milk and a brightness from lime juice. This makes a lot, but I always freeze half of it to pull out for a last-minute dinner gathering or to bring to a party.

MAKES 16 SERVINGS

PRESSURE COOKER INGREDIENTS

2½ cups (570 ml) water

1 cup (200 g) unsoaked chickpeas

FOOD PROCESSOR INGREDIENTS

1 (13.6-oz [403-ml]) can full-fat coconut milk

1–2 tbsp (8–16 g) Thai red curry paste, to taste

2 tbsp (30 ml) lime juice

Salt, to taste

For the pressure cooker, add the water and chickpeas to your Instant Pot. Put on the lid and close the pressure valve. Cook on high pressure for 45 minutes.

Let the pressure release naturally.

For the food processor, strain the chickpeas and add to the processor along with the coconut milk, curry paste (start with 1 tablespoon [8 g] and add more later if desired) and lime juice. Blend until smooth, then add salt to taste.

PER ¼-CUP (50-G) SERVING: Calories 61.0, protein 1.0 g, total fat 4.4 g, carbohydrates 4.2 g, sodium 66.8 mg, fiber 0.7 g

Technically, this recipe has no added refined oil, but we all know that coconut milk is high in fat. If you are on a no- or restricted-oil diet, you can always use unsweetened coconut milk from a carton, like So Delicious, and a little coconut extract to get a similar flavor with fewer calories.

BLACK BEAN QUINOA BURGERS

gluten-free, soy-free, no added oil option*

Every vegan needs a quick and easy bean burger in his or her repertoire. For this one you toss the long-cooking ingredients into your pressure cooker, then mix the spices and flaxseed in. I like to freeze at least half of these for an impromptu dinner party another night.

MAKES 12 PATTIES

SAUTÉ INGREDIENTS

1 tbsp (15 ml) oil (or *dry sauté or add a little water/vegetable broth)

½ cup (80 g) chopped onion

8 cloves garlic, minced

PRESSURE COOKER INGREDIENTS

1 cup (184 g) dried unsoaked black beans or pinto beans

½ cup (85 g) quinoa, rinsed well

½ cup (79 g) brown rice

4 cups (946 ml) water

PATTY INGREDIENTS

½ cup (90 g) ground flaxseed

1 tbsp (2 g) dried marjoram

2 tsp (12 g) salt (or to taste if you are limiting your intake)

2 tsp (4 g) smoked paprika

1 tsp pepper

1 tsp dried thyme

For the sauté, use the sauté setting over normal, or medium heat, and heat the oil or broth. Add the onion and sauté until transparent, 5 minutes. Then add the garlic and sauté a minute more.

For the pressure cooker, add the black beans, quinoa, rice and water to the onion mixture and stir to combine. Put the lid on and make sure the steam release handle is set to sealing, or closed; cook on high pressure for 34 minutes.

Carefully move the pressure valve and release the pressure manually.

Preheat your oven to 350°F (180°C, or gas mark 4) and prepare 2 baking sheets with parchment paper.

For the patties, mash the beans in the pot, then mix in the ground flaxseed, marjoram, salt, paprika, pepper and thyme. If the mix is too loose, turn on the sauté function and cook uncovered until the extra water evaporates.

Divide the mixture into 12 portions (about a heaping ⅓ cup [80 g] each), form into patties and place on the baking sheet.

Note: If your mixture is still too wet to form into patties, add some brown rice or whole wheat flour 1 tablespoon (8 g) at a time until the dough is thick enough to work with.

Cook for 20 minutes on one side, then carefully flip and cook for 10–15 minutes more, or until they have firmed up.

Serve as a main course with steamed veggies on the side or on a bun with all the fixings.

PER SERVING: Calories 90.4, protein 3.7 g, total fat 3.3 g, carbohydrates 12.7 g, sodium 2.8 mg, fiber 3.4 g

These freeze well and are wonderful to have on hand. You can even vary the spices to keep them interesting.

CHAPTER 4

Fun and Delicious Ways to Add in More Whole Grains

This is another pillar of a plant-based diet. Whole grains are full of fiber and vitamins, not to mention they help keep you full.

Some people pass up on brown rice or long-cooking grains like Kamut or oat groats because it can take an hour or more on the stove. In your Instant Pot it will take half the time. In fact, you can cook quinoa or steel-cut oats in 3 minutes.

Long-cooking grains have their own special setting on the Instant Pot. They will still cook for a long time, but all of that time is hands off. So do some errands, tidy up or read a book and have a glass of wine or cup of herbal tea. Dinner will let you know when it's ready.

WHOLE GRAINS COOKING CHART

Different kinds of grains weigh vastly different amounts, so make sure you measure by volume, not weight.

QUICK-COOKING GRAINS

TYPE	TIME	1 CUP GRAIN TO X CUPS WATER OR BROTH
Amaranth	5 minutes	2¼ cups (530 ml) liquid
Pearled Barley	20 minutes	2 cups (470 ml) liquid
Millet	10 minutes	1½ cups (355 ml) liquid
Quinoa	3 minutes	1½ cups (355 ml) liquid
Rolled Oats (cooked in ramekins inside pressure cooker)	4 minutes	2 cups (470 ml) liquid
Sorghum	35 minutes	2½ cups (590 ml) liquid
Steel-Cut Oats	3 minutes	3 cups (700 ml) liquid

RICE

TYPE	TIME	1 CUP GRAIN TO X CUPS WATER OR BROTH
Arborio Rice	6–8 minutes	3 cups (700 ml) liquid
Black Forbidden Rice	15 minutes	1½ cups (355 ml) liquid
Brown Rice	23 minutes	1½ cups (355 ml) liquid
Pink Rice	10 minutes	1¼ cups (300 ml) liquid
Red Rice	10 minutes	2 cups (470 ml) liquid
Sushi Rice	6 minutes	1 cup (235 ml) liquid
White Rice	4 minutes	1 cup (235 ml) liquid or use the rice function/ button on the Instant Pot

LONG-COOKING GRAINS

These grains are usually soaked overnight before cooking. These are also a great choice for slow cooking overnight.

Barley (not pearled), farro, Kamut, oat groats and wheat berries can be cooked with a special long-cooking multigrain function. See the method on page 93 for Perfect Kamut (and other long-cooking grains).

PERFECT KAMUT (AND OTHER LONG-COOKING GRAINS)

gluten-free option*, soy-free, no added oil

Kamut, also known as Khorasan wheat, is an ancient variety of wheat. Some people with wheat sensitivity have been known to tolerate it, but do be aware that it contains gluten. It's a delicious and hearty grain that can be used as a base in a bowl or a grain salad.

The main reason I don't cook Kamut much is that you need to soak it before cooking. I've managed to avoid that by cooking it in the slow cooker. However, in the spirit of this book, I tried to soak some, and still managed to forget about it. There is a magic setting on the Instant Pot that solves this problem for me. It's part of the multigrain button program that defaults to 40 minutes on high pressure. However, if you press the adjust button once, it will look like it's going to cook a normal 60 minutes. But on this setting—only on the multigrain 60-minute cycle—the grain first gets a 45-minute warm water soaking time before the 60 minutes of pressure cooking time. It's perfectly cooked and you can't leave it soaking for too long!

MAKES 6 SERVINGS

3 cups (700 ml) water or broth

1 cup (186 g) Kamut (*make gluten-free version with oat groats or sorghum)

Place the water and Kamut in your Instant Pot, put on the lid and set to sealing, or close the steam release handle. Click the multigrain button, then click the adjust button 1 time. This starts a special setting that will soak the grain in warm water for 45 minutes before it begins the 60-minute pressure cooking cycle.

After it's finished cooking let the pressure release naturally. If there's too much water, change to the sauté setting and let the extra liquid evaporate.

PER SERVING: Calories 201.2, protein 7.8 g, total fat 2.2 g, carbohydrates 37.9 g, sodium 10.6 mg, fiber 4.5 g

This long-cooking setting also cooks wheat berries, spelt and oat groats to perfection.

ROLLED OAT RAMEKINS

gluten-free*, soy-free, no added oil

Steel-cut oats are great in your Instant Pot, but what if you only have rolled oats in your pantry?
Make oatmeal in ramekins! Cooking them over a rack slows the cooking time enough to not make mush
of your oats. You'll need four 8- or 9-ounce (225- or 253-g) ramekins.

MAKES 4 SERVINGS

1⅓ cups (124 g) rolled oats, divided (*make sure the oats are labeled gluten-free)

2⅔ cups (635 ml) water, divided

Sweetener of choice, to taste (optional)

4 big pinches of ground cinnamon (optional)

Add the rack and 1½ cups (355 ml) of water to your Instant Pot. In each ramekin mix ⅓ cup (31 g) rolled oats, ⅔ cup (160 ml) water and any optional ingredients that you are using.

Cover each ramekin with foil and stack on the rack.

Cook on high pressure for 4 minutes and release the pressure naturally. Carefully remove the hot ramekins with tongs or small silicone finger pot holders.

PER SERVING: Calories 99.8, protein 3.3 g, total fat 2.0 g, carbohydrates 18.0 g, sodium 0.0 mg, fiber 2.7 g

Use this recipe as a starting place and add in your favorite dried fruits, spices and even fresh fruit!

VEGAN SUSHI BOWL

gluten-free option, soy-free, no added oil

This is my favorite summer meal. It's so much easier to make than actual sushi—no rolling required. Plus, Cheryl won't eat nori, so this works for her, too. Even though the sushi rice stays the same, you can use a variety of steamed veggies and other toppings to keep it new and exciting. This dish makes a great buffet dish because diners can select their favorite toppings!

MAKES 6 SERVINGS

INSTANT POT INGREDIENTS

2 cups (400 g) white sushi rice

2 cups (475 ml) water

AFTER COOKING INGREDIENTS

⅓ cup (80 ml) rice vinegar

2 tbsp (28 g) vegan sugar

½ tsp salt

For the Instant Pot, add the rice and water to the Instant Pot and cook on high pressure for 6 minutes. Carefully open the pressure valve and manually release the pressure.

Scrape the rice out into a large stainless steel bowl.

After cooking, add the vinegar, sugar and salt to the dirty Instant Pot liner, turn to sauté and heat just enough to melt the sugar.

Pour the vinegar mixture over the rice and use the rice paddle that came with your Instant Pot to keep moving the rice around until it has cooled. You can store this in the fridge for up to 3 days.

PER SERVING: Calories 277.8, protein 3.8 g, total fat 0.0 g, carbohydrates 61.9 g, sodium 200.0 mg, fiber 0.0 g

Make a brown rice version by using 1½ cups (285 g) short-grain brown rice and 1¾ cups (415 ml) water. Cook on high pressure for 22 minutes and let the pressure release naturally. Add ½ cup (120 ml) rice vinegar after cooking.

SESAME CUCUMBER TOPPING

gluten-free option**, soy-free option*, no oil added option***

3 cups (312 g) cubed cucumbers

1 tbsp (15 ml) soy sauce (or *use coconut aminos or **make sure soy sauce is labeled gluten-free)

1 tbsp (15 ml) seasoned rice vinegar

1 tsp sesame oil (***leave out to make oil-free or use 1 tbsp [8 g] toasted sesame seeds)

Mix everything in a bowl and store in the fridge until you are ready to serve.

PER SERVING: Calories 19.4, protein 0.6 g, total fat 0.9 g, carbohydrates 2.5 g, sodium 191.7 mg, fiber 0.5 g

SPICY TOMATO TOPPING

gluten-free, soy-free, no added oil option*

3 cups (540 g) chopped fresh tomatoes

1 tbsp (18 g) vegan mayonnaise (or *leave out or use the oil-free cauliflower sour cream on page 40)

1 tbsp (15 g) Sriracha or less if you don't want it very spicy

1 tbsp (15 ml) seasoned rice vinegar

Pinch of salt (optional)

Mix everything in a bowl and store in the fridge until you are ready to serve.

PER SERVING: Calories 39.7, protein 0.8 g, total fat 2.0 g, carbohydrates 5.6 g, sodium 110.6 mg, fiber 1.0 g

MORE TOPPING IDEAS

Steamed julienned veggies such as carrots

Sliced avocado

Sprouts

Sliced pickled ginger

UTTAPAM WITH CILANTRO COCONUT CHUTNEY

gluten-free, soy-free, no added oil option*

Uttapams are savory South Indian pancakes. It gets a wonderful crispy outside while retaining a tender inside. For me, it's a perfect meal anytime of the day once you add some Cilantro Coconut Chutney.

MAKES 12 UTTAPAMS

1 cup (151 g) urad dal (skinned split urad)

1 cup (190 g) brown rice

1 cup (119 g) millet

1 cup (170 g) quinoa, washed well to remove the seed coating

5 cups (1.2 L) water

Spray oil (optional)*

TOPPINGS

Grated carrots

Grated summer squash

Chopped cilantro

Peas

Shredded vegan cheese

Leftover curries

Mix the urad dal, rice, millet, quinoa and water in a large bowl. Cover and let soak to soften for 8 hours.

Next, puree the mixture in your blender in batches and add to your Instant Pot liner. Place the liner in your Instant Pot, cover and press the yogurt setting. Leave it at the default 8 hours for it to ferment.

You can store the fermented mixture in your fridge for up to 1 week or you can cook up all the pancakes at once and freeze them to heat for later.

Coat a large skillet with nonstick spray oil (if using) and place over medium heat. Once hot, add ½ cup (120 ml) of the batter per pancake and shape into a circle. Cook until bubbles begin to form.

Sprinkle the topping you choose over the top of the pancake and press in a little with your spatula. Flip the pancake and cook until both sides are browned.

Place on a plate and cook the next one. You could also have more than one skillet going at a time.

PER SERVING WITHOUT OIL: Calories 103.6, protein 3.8 g, total fat 1.1 g, carbohydrates 20.2 g, sodium 6.1 mg, fiber 2.1 g

CILANTRO COCONUT CHUTNEY

1 cup (93 g) shredded coconut

½ cup (120 ml) water

½ cup (8 g) fresh cilantro (leaves and stems)

1 tbsp (6 g) grated ginger

1 tbsp (6 g) curry leaves (optional)

2 tsp (10 ml) lemon juice

1 tsp salt

⅛ tsp mustard powder

Place all the ingredients into your blender and pulverize. You will need to scrape down a few times and may need to add an additional tablespoon or two (15 or 30 ml) of water.

Store in the fridge for up to 1 week.

PER SERVING: Calories 24.0, protein 0.2 g, total fat 2.2 g, carbohydrates 1.1 g, sodium 1.4 mg, fiber 0.6 g

OIL-FREE PUMPKIN TAMALES

gluten-free, soy-free, no added oil

I've been in love with Mexican food for a long time and have been cooking more and more of it these days. I knew that tamales would be perfect for the Instant Pot. Many tamales are full of oil, but these keep their moisture by using pumpkin, and it gives them a great flavor, too. You can easily double this recipe if you want.

MAKES 12 TAMALES

1 (15-oz [425-g]) can pumpkin puree or 1½ cups (375 g) homemade

2 tsp (2 g) dried oregano

1½ tsp (1.5 g) ground cumin

1 tsp ground chipotle pepper (or less to make it less spicy)

1 tsp baking powder

1 tsp salt

2 cups (228 g) corn masa

1½ cups (355 ml) water

12 corn husks, soaked in warm water for at least 2 hours, drained

Cauliflower Sour Cream (page 40), optional

Mole Sauce (page 105), optional

Salsa, optional

Add the pumpkin, oregano, cumin, chipotle, baking powder and salt to your mixer (or mixing bowl). Mix until everything is incorporated.

Put the masa in a medium-size mixing bowl, add the water and mix well. Add the masa mixture to the pumpkin mixture in golf-ball-sized balls while the mixer is running. This will create a fluffier mixture and the texture should be like a soft playdough.

Put a steamer or mesh insert in your Instant Pot and add 1½ cups (355 ml) water.

Set up a workstation with a cutting board, the tamale batter and the corn husks. Put ⅓ cup (80 g) tamale batter in the top half of the corn husk and spread into a thick rectangle that goes to the top (or wide part) of the husk. I do this with a spatula so that I can scrape the dough into the shape I want.

Fold the pointed end up to the top, fold one side over the other and tightly roll it into a flat tube. Place with the open side up in the steamer and repeat until all the batter is used.

Cook on high pressure for 23 minutes and let the pressure release naturally.

Serve topped with Cauliflower Sour Cream, Mole Sauce or your favorite salsa.

PER SERVING WITHOUT TOPPING: Calories 80.8, protein 2.1 g, total fat 0.7 g, carbohydrates 17.3 g, sodium 42.9 mg, fiber 1.1 g

MOLE SAUCE

gluten-free, soy-free, no added oil

I love mole sauce because of its depth of flavor. The chiles and spices together add fruity notes. It's a complex taste, but making it is easy. You can find dried chiles at most grocery stores, any Hispanic market and on the Internet. You just toast the chiles, then reconstitute them, then blend with the other ingredients and you have the most amazing sauce that you will want to slather on everything!

MAKES ABOUT 3 CUPS (700 ML)

PRESSURE COOKER INGREDIENTS

4 dried guajillo chiles

3 or 4 dried ancho chiles (you want the same amount of pepper from each kind)

3 cups (700 ml) water

BLENDER INGREDIENTS

½ cup (73 g) blanched almonds

3 tbsp (15 g) nutritional yeast

3 tbsp (16 g) cocoa powder

1 tbsp (14 g) coconut sugar or brown sugar

2 tsp (2 g) dried oregano

1½ tsp (7 g) salt

1 tsp granulated garlic

½ tsp ground cumin

¼ tsp ground allspice

¼ tsp ground cinnamon

1 cup (235 ml) chile cooking water

1 cup (235 ml) plain water (or use all chile water)

For the pressure cooker, cut or tear the chiles in half and remove the stems and seeds (wear gloves for this). Tear the remaining flesh into equal-size pieces so they will cook evenly. Use the sauté setting over low, and toast until they become fragrant and dry.

Add the 3 cups (700 ml) water to the pot with the chiles and cook on high pressure for 5 minutes. Let the pressure release naturally.

For the blender, while the chiles are cooking, add the almonds, nutritional yeast, cocoa powder, sugar, oregano, salt, garlic, cumin, allspice and cinnamon to your blender and blend until the almonds break down.

Use tongs to remove the reconstituted chile pieces and put them into the blender. Carefully ladle out 1 cup (235 ml) of the chile cooking water and add the 1 cup (235 ml) plain water to the blender and blend until smooth.

This is amazing on the Oil-Free Pumpkin Tamales (page 102)—you have to try it.

PER ½-CUP (120-ML) SERVING: Calories 132.8, protein 6.4 g, total fat 7.5 g, carbohydrates 14.0 g, sodium 5.6 mg, fiber 5.9 g

Save any leftover cooking water from the chiles and use it instead of water to make tamales or homemade tortillas!

Mole is not a very spicy sauce by nature. However, you can add in a few hot dried peppers such as mora, chipotle or arbol if you want it spicy.

TAMALES MADE WITH COCONUT OIL

gluten-free, soy-free, no added oil option*

This is as close to a traditional tamale that you could get if they had vegan ones. Traditionally, they are made with lard, but coconut oil does a better job and adds a great flavor. You can fill these with leftover black beans (page 24), Spicy Jackfruit Tinga (page 145) or your favorite store-bought vegan chorizo.

MAKES 12 TAMALES

¾ cup (164 g) coconut oil, warmed (or *use pumpkin or sweet potato puree)

1 tsp baking powder

½ tsp salt

2 cups (228 g) corn masa

1½ cups (355 ml) water or broth

About 1 cup (240 g) choice of filling

12 corn husks, soaked in warm water for at least 2 hours, drained

FILLING OPTIONS

Vegan cheese

Vegan chorizo

Vegan ground meat

Black or pinto beans

Salsa

Corn

Green chiles

Shredded carrots and zucchini

Mushroom Potato Taco Filling (page 142)

Spicy Jackfruit Tinga (page 145)

The Best Not-Refried Black Beans (page 24)

Tomatillo-Poblano White Beans (page 70)

Cauliflower Sour Cream (page 40)

Mole Sauce (page 105)

Vegan Cauliflower Queso (page 138)

Salsa

Add the coconut oil, baking powder and salt to your mixer (or mixing bowl). Mix for a couple of minutes until everything is incorporated and fluffy.

Put the masa in a medium-sized mixing bowl, add the water and mix well. Add the masa mixture to the pumpkin mixture in golf-ball-sized balls while the mixer is running. This will create a fluffier mixture and the texture should be like a soft playdough.

Put a steamer or mesh insert into your Instant Pot and add 1½ cups (355 ml) water.

Set up a workstation with a cutting board, the tamale batter and the corn husks. Put ⅓ cup (80 ml) tamale batter in the top half of the corn husk and spread into a thin rectangle that goes to the top (or wide part) of the husk. I do this with a spatula so that I can scrape the dough into the shape I want.

In the middle, add a tablespoon (15 g) of your filling choice. Roll the entire tamale over while pressing it firmly together, similar to how you would roll a burrito. As you roll the tamale the top part of the husk will go slightly underneath the other edge as you complete the roll. Pull the husk back to make sure the corn dough enveloped the filling.

Fold the pointy end of the corn husk up and place with the open side up in the steamer. Repeat with each tamale until all the batter is used. Cook on high pressure for 20 minutes and let the pressure release naturally.

Serve topped with Cauliflower Sour Cream, Mole Sauce, Vegan Cauliflower Queso or your favorite salsa.

PER TAMALE WITH CORN FILLING: Calories 198.0, protein 2.2 g, total fat 14.5 g, carbohydrates 17.0 g, sodium 43.5 mg, fiber 0.3 g

WHOLE-GRAIN CORNBREAD

gluten-free option*, soy-free, no added oil option**

Sometimes beans are just not enough on their own. This cornbread can be cooked on a rack above the Southern-Style Pinto Beans on page 73 and will make a complete meal. This will be a heavier cornbread than you might be used to because it's steamed in the Instant Pot.

MAKES 8 SERVINGS

DRY INGREDIENTS

1½ cups (236 g) cornmeal

1 cup (120 g) whole wheat flour (or *use a gluten-free baking mix)

2 tsp (5 g) jalapeño or ground chile powder (optional)

¾ tsp baking soda

¼ tsp salt

WET INGREDIENTS

1½ cups (360 ml) unsweetened nondairy milk

2 tbsp (10 g) ground flaxseed mixed with 4 tbsp (60 ml) warm water

1 tbsp (15 ml) oil (or **use pumpkin puree)

For the dry ingredients, mix the cornmeal, flour, jalapeño powder, baking soda and salt in a small mixing bowl, then set aside.

For the wet ingredients, mix the nondairy milk, flaxseed mixture and oil in a large mixing bowl. Add the dry mix to the wet one and stir well.

Oil a 7-inch (17.5-cm) springform pan that fits into your Instant Pot, or an 8-inch (20-cm) cake pan with a removable bottom. Make sure to try to fit the pan in your Instant Pot on the rack BEFORE you pour in the batter.

Pour in the batter and spread evenly. Add the rack to your Instant Pot and add 1½ cups (355 ml) water.

If your pan does not fit inside the rack handles, you will need to fashion some handles out of aluminum foil to lower the pan into the cooker. Tear off two pieces of foil about 3 feet (1 m) long, fold each one lengthwise two times. Lay the foil handles out on the counter in a plus sign near your cooker. Place your pan in the center, where the two pieces cross. Pull the handles up and carefully lift the pan into your Instant Pot.

Place the lid on with the steam release handle closed and cook on high pressure for 40 minutes. Let the pressure release naturally. Once the pressure indicator goes down, remove the lid, lift out the pan using the foil handles and remove the foil that's covering the pan.

PER SERVING: Calories 168.8, protein 4.7 g, total fat 4.5 g, carbohydrates 30.2 g, sodium 164.0 mg, fiber 4.6 g

CHAPTER 5

Eat Your Vegetables: Easy and Elegant Plant-Based Fare

You may not think about cooking your vegetables in the pressure cooker during the winter. It can be nice to heat up the house by cooking everything on the stove or in the oven. But even in the winter I bet you'd still like to eat "baked" potatoes in 15 minutes or have a stew in less than 30 minutes.

On the flip side of that is summer. Your counter is layered with beautiful veggies from your CSA or farmers' market. If you're like me, you don't grill and there's no way you want to turn on the oven or stove. The Instant Pot comes to the rescue!

The Quick and Easy Summer Vegetable Plate on page 125 is the quintessential Southern summer vegetable plate. Fresh corn on the cob, green beans and summer squash—each with its own flavor—will come out of your one Instant Pot.

Some people who use stove-top pressure cookers only are not fans of cooking vegetables in an electric pressure cooker. But there are those of us who disagree.

There are a few tricks to keep in mind when cooking vegetables. One is that if you feel your veggies are cooked more than to your liking you can always use the low-pressure setting.

But what if 1 minute is too much? Set it for 0 minutes—yes, zero minutes—it's not a typo. What happens is that the vegetables still get cooked as the heat brings the pot up to pressure, then again until the pressure release. Pretty awesome, right?

Remember to cut your vegetables uniformly so they can all cook evenly. You can also cut long-cooking vegetables smaller than quick-cooking ones to cook them together.

Another trick is to cook in layers. Wrap the quick-cooking vegetables in foil or put in a foil-covered baking dish and place on top of the other food in the pot. The vegetables will cook slower when they are closer to the top.

You can cook frozen vegetables in your Instant Pot, too; just try adding 1 minute to the time for cooking fresh.

VEGETABLE COOKING CHART

LONG-COOKING VEGETABLES

I think of large whole vegetables as being long cooking. They are also great to layer on the bottom of the Instant Pot. Use high pressure unless otherwise noted.

NAME OF VEGETABLE	SIZE	TIME
Beets	medium whole	15 minutes
White Baking Potato	medium whole	15 minutes
Baby Potatoes	whole	10 minutes
Turnips	whole	8 minutes
Sweet Potatoes	medium whole	15 minutes
Winter Squash	medium whole	15 minutes

QUICK-COOKING VEGETABLES

These will vary depending on age, thickness and other factors, but here are a few starting points to try cooking them. Use high pressure unless otherwise noted.

NAME OF VEGETABLE	SIZE	TIME
Asparagus	medium whole	1 minute
Broccoli	florets	2 minutes
Brussels Sprouts	baby	2 minutes
Brussels Sprouts	large	3 minutes
Carrots	sliced	2 minutes
Cauliflower	florets	2 minutes
Green Beans	whole or half	2 minutes
Greens	whole or chopped	2 minutes
Peas	medium whole	2 minutes
Summer Squash	medium whole	0 minutes

WHOLE SPAGHETTI SQUASH

gluten-free, soy-free, no added oil

This is one cool Instant Pot trick! Of course, make sure the squash you buy will fit in your Instant Pot, but other than that it's so simple. There's no cutting or peeling, and you don't even poke holes in it because the pressure pushes it together. The best part of all is the skin slips right off after cooking!

MAKES 2–4 SERVINGS

1 whole spaghetti squash, washed well (about 1 lb [453 g])

Place the rack in your Instant Pot and add 1½ cups (355 ml) water. Place the squash on the rack and cook on high pressure for 15 minutes and let the pressure release naturally.

Once the squash is cool enough to touch, peel off the skin. Cut in half widthwise and scoop out the seeds with a spoon. Cut off the stem.

You will be able to start pulling the strands out. I just mash the softest outside parts with my hands so it will get disguised in the sauce I use.

PER 1-CUP (250-G) SERVING: Calories 41.9, protein 1.0 g, total fat 0.4 g, carbohydrates 10.0 g, sodium 27.9 mg, fiber 2.2 g

If you usually cut your spaghetti squash lengthwise, you're in for a surprise. The way the strands grow, cutting it lengthwise is like breaking your spaghetti noodles in half. By cutting it widthwise you'll have the longest strands.

You can cook all winter squash and pumpkins just like this in your Instant Pot. Of course, make sure they fit and adjust the time up if they are dense. You can always put the lid back on and add extra cooking time if it's not done from the first cooking.

NOT-BAKED POTATOES

gluten-free, soy-free, no added oil

Baked potatoes are filling, full of nutrition and one of my favorite comfort foods! You can cook up some on the spot or cook a batch ahead of time. Eat it as is or serve a stew or chili over it. I love to top it with the Vegan Cauliflower Queso on page 138 and lots of steamed seasonal vegetables.

MAKES 4 SERVINGS

4 whole baking potatoes, washed well

Place the rack in your Instant Pot and add 1½ cups (355 ml) water. Place the potatoes on the rack and cook on high pressure for 15–30 minutes depending on their size: if the potatoes are fairly small, start them at 15 minutes; if they are really large, begin at 30 minutes. You can always put the lid back on and cook for more time if they aren't done when you test them with a fork.

Let the pressure release naturally.

PER POTATO: Calories 160.4, protein 4.3 g, total fat 0.2 g, carbohydrates 36.5 g, sodium 17.3 mg, fiber 3.8 g

Make it a meal by cutting the potato in half and ladling one of these over it:
DIY Vegan Ricotta (page 39)
Smoky Pecan Brussels Sprouts (page 121)
The Best Not-Refried Black Beans (page 24) and Mole Sauce (page 105)
Spicy Jackfruit Tinga (page 145)

NOT-BAKED SWEET POTATOES

gluten-free, soy-free, no added oil

Sweet potatoes are delicious and full of nutritional goodness. You can make a batch for a side dish, serve a savory stew over it or turn it into dessert!

MAKES 4 SERVINGS

4 whole sweet potatoes, washed well

Place the rack in your Instant Pot and add 1½ cups (355 ml) water. Place the sweet potatoes on the rack and cook on high pressure for 10–20 minutes depending on their size: if the sweet potatoes are fairly thin, start them at 10 minutes; if they are really large, begin at 20 minutes.

Let the pressure release naturally.

PER POTATO: Calories 136.5, protein 2.1 g, total fat 0.4 g, carbohydrates 31.6 g, sodium 16.9 mg, fiber 3.9 g

Make it savory by cutting it in half and ladling one of these over it:
Kidney Bean Étouffée (page 78)
Southern-Style Pinto Beans (page 73)
Lots O' Veggies Bolognese (page 137)
Spicy Jackfruit Tinga (page 145)

Make it into dessert with:
Chai Applesauce (page 48)
Date Caramel Filling (page 197)
Creamy Coconut Sauce (below)
Or top it with vegan chocolate chips and vegan marshmallows and stick in the oven at 350°F (180°C, or gas mark 4) for 10 minutes.

CREAMY COCONUT SAUCE

MAKES 12 SERVINGS

1 (15.5-oz [400-ml]) can full-fat coconut milk

½ cup (110 g) coconut sugar

Heat the coconut milk and sugar in a saucepan over medium heat, whisking every few minutes. Cook until the mixture has reduced by one-third to one-half, or your desired thickness. This sauce will thicken as it cools.

PER 2-TABLESPOON (30 ML) SERVING: Calories 267.3, protein 0.5 g, total fat 5.7 g, carbohydrates 9.3 g, sodium 0.0 mg, fiber 0.0 g

SMOKY PECAN BRUSSELS SPROUTS

gluten-free, soy-free, no added oil

This recipe will turn your sprout haters into spout devourers! I used a variation of this to get Cheryl to try sprouts for the first time. The sweet and smoky flavor really make these Brussels sprouts addictive.

MAKES 4 SIDE DISH SERVINGS

PRESSURE COOKER INGREDIENTS

2 cups (176 g) small baby Brussels sprouts, as close to the same size as possible

¼ cup (60 ml) water

½ tsp liquid smoke

SAUTÉ INGREDIENTS

¼ cup (28 g) chopped pecans

2 tbsp (30 ml) maple syrup

Salt, to taste

For the pressure cooker, add the Brussels sprouts, water and liquid smoke to your Instant Pot and mix well. Put the lid on and close the pressure valve. Cook on high pressure for 2 minutes. (Note: If you have very large Brussels sprouts, you may need to double the cooking time.)

Once the cooking time is up, carefully move the pressure release valve to release the pressure manually.

For the sauté, switch to the sauté function and add in the pecans and maple syrup and reduce the liquid as you finish cooking the sprouts. Remove from the heat once tender and add salt to taste.

PER SERVING: Calories 96.4, protein 2.2 g, total fat 5.5 g, carbohydrates 11.7 g, sodium 11.9 mg, fiber 2.4 g

Brussels sprouts vary greatly in size. Do your best to pick ones close in size or cut the largest ones in half. You can use frozen sprouts in this recipe; just up the cooking time by a minute or two depending on their size.

JILL NUSSINOW'S LEMONY ENGLISH PEAS AND ASPARAGUS

gluten-free, soy-free, no added oil

Spring vegetables are some of my friend Jill Nussinow's favorites, and mine too. You probably know Jill from her new book, *Vegan Under Pressure*, or as the Veggie Queen (TheVeggieQueen.com). This is the perfect side dish, but you can make a whole meal out of it with a hearty side of your favorite whole grain or pasta.

MAKES 4 SERVINGS

1–2 cloves garlic, minced

2 cups (268 g) fresh English peas (frozen unthawed)

2 cups (268 g) asparagus, cut into 1–2" (2.5–5-cm) pieces

¼ cup (60 ml) vegetable broth

Zest and juice of 1 lemon

2–3 tbsp (10–14 g) pine nuts or slivered almonds, toasted

Add the garlic, peas, asparagus and broth to the pressure cooker. Put on the lid and close the pressure valve. Cook on low pressure for 2 minutes.

When time is up, manually release the pressure. Add the lemon zest and juice and stir. Transfer to a bowl or plate. Garnish with the nuts.

PER SERVING: Calories 104.1, protein 6.5 g, total fat 2.1 g, carbohydrates 16.9 g, sodium 318.7 mg, fiber 6.3 g

Can't find fresh peas? Don't worry, you can use frozen peas, just cook for 1 minute less.

QUICK AND EASY SUMMER VEGETABLE PLATE

gluten-free, soy-free, no added oil

If you get some corn, green beans and summer squash at the market or in your CSA, you can make this perfect summer meal of lime corn, smoked green beans and herbed squash. There will be no sweating over the stove. I recommend serving this with thick-sliced ripe tomatoes chopped and tossed in balsamic vinegar.

MAKES 4 SERVINGS

BOTTOM LAYER INGREDIENTS

4 large ears corn, shucked and cleaned

1 cup (237 ml) water

1 lime

Salt, as needed

MIDDLE LAYER INGREDIENTS

4 cups (400 g) green beans, broken in half if large

½ tsp liquid smoke

¼–½ tsp salt, to taste

TOP LAYER INGREDIENTS

2 medium summer squash, sliced

2 tbsp (3 g) chopped fresh thyme, basil and oregano (or use a salt-free dried blend of your choice)

For the bottom layer, arrange the corn in the Instant Pot liner and pour in the water.

For the middle layer, sprinkle the green beans with the liquid smoke and salt, then seal in a foil packet and set on top of the corn.

For the top layer, toss the squash and herbs together, then seal in a foil packet and place on top of the green bean layer.

Cook on high pressure for 10 minutes. Let the pressure release naturally. Once the pressure indicator goes down, remove the lid and carefully lift out the packets.

Before serving, squeeze lime juice on the corn and sprinkle with salt, or serve with lime wedges and let your guests do it themselves.

PER SERVING: Calories 178.1, protein 7.9 g, total fat 2.0 g, carbohydrates 40.2 g, sodium 31.6 mg, fiber 9.2 g

HEALTHY CREAM OF ASPARAGUS SOUP

gluten-free, soy-free, no added oil option*

Why yes, this is an oil-free creamy soup that has no nuts. You may be worrying about cooking the smaller asparagus tips, but by wrapping them in foil or putting them in a Pyrex container covered with foil you slow the cooking process.

MAKES 4 SERVINGS

SAUTÉ INGREDIENTS

1 tbsp (15 ml) mild oil (or *dry sauté or add a little water/vegetable broth)

½ cup (80 g) minced onion

½ tsp minced garlic

PRESSURE COOKER INGREDIENTS

1 lb (453 g) asparagus, ends and tips snapped off

3 cups (321 g) cauliflower florets

3 cups (700 ml) water

1 vegetable bouillon cube

1 tsp thyme

1" (2.5-cm) strip lemon peel

1 bay leaf

BLENDER INGREDIENTS

1 tbsp (5 g) nutritional yeast

⅛ tsp nutmeg

Salt and pepper, to taste

For the sauté, use the sauté setting over normal, or medium heat, and heat the oil or broth. Add the onion and sauté until transparent, 5 minutes. Then add the garlic and sauté for 2 more minutes.

Add the asparagus (except for the tips), cauliflower, water, bouillon cube, thyme, lemon peel and bay leaf and mix well. Place the asparagus tips in a foil packet and place on top of the asparagus mixture. Put the lid on and make sure the steam release handle is set to sealing, or closed; change to the manual setting on high and set the timer for 2 minutes.

Carefully move the pressure valve to steam release handle and release the pressure manually. Set the foil packet aside for serving. Discard the bay leaf and lemon peel.

For the blender, transfer the cooked asparagus and cauliflower mixture to your blender along with the nutritional yeast and nutmeg. Blend until smooth and season with salt and pepper to taste.

Serve topped with the asparagus tips.

PER SERVING: Calories 93.9, protein 5.1 g, total fat 3.9 g, carbohydrates 11.4 g, sodium 25.4 mg, fiber 4.9 g

If you have a delicate veggie or one that will cook faster than the main mixture, you can always wrap it in foil and put it at the top and it will cook slower.

INDO-CHINESE CORN SOUP

gluten-free, soy-free, no added oil

I was introduced to Indo-Chinese food a few years ago. Just like our American Chinese restaurants changed to fit our tastes, there were changes made to suit the Indian palate. The food tends to feature some Indian spices and is much less sweet than American Chinese food. This soup has a bit of cumin in it with lots of ginger, which sets it apart from the rest.

MAKES 4 SERVINGS

5 cups (1.2 L) vegetable broth (or water with a bouillon cube)

2½ cups (440 g) corn kernels

1 cup (128 g) minced carrot

1 cup (89 g) minced cabbage

1 tbsp (15 ml) soy sauce

2 tsp (9 g) sesame oil

2 tsp (8 g) grated ginger

2 tsp (6 g) minced garlic

1½ tsp (3 g) ground cumin

Ground pepper, to taste

Add the broth, corn, carrot, cabbage, soy sauce, sesame oil, ginger, garlic and cumin to your Instant Pot.

Cook on high pressure for 10 minutes. Let the pressure release naturally.

Blend about 3 cups (700 ml) of the soup to thicken and return to the soup. Taste, add pepper and reseason as needed.

PER SERVING: Calories 163.8, protein 5.3 g, total fat 3.5 g, carbohydrates 29.8 g, sodium 841.3 mg, fiber 5.3 g

SNOWY DAY POTATO CABBAGE SOUP

gluten-free, soy-free, no added oil option*

In the South, if snow is predicted there is a mad dash to the store for milk, bread and toilet paper. While everyone else is hurrying to the grocery store, you can stay in your jammies and make this filling Slavic-inspired potato cabbage soup. Your calm house will be filled with the smells of caraway seeds, paprika and dill.

MAKES 6 SERVINGS

SAUTÉ INGREDIENTS

1 tbsp (15 ml) mild oil (or *dry sauté or add a little water/vegetable broth)

2 cups (174 g) minced onion

1½ tsp (4 g) minced garlic

1½ tsp (3 g) caraway seeds

1 tsp smoked or plain paprika

PRESSURE COOKER INGREDIENTS

8 cups (1893 ml) water

4 cups (680 g) chopped cabbage

4 cups (624 g) cubed potatoes

2 cups (256 g) sliced carrots

1 vegetable bouillon cube

1½ tsp (1.5 g) dried dill

BEFORE SERVING

½ cup (48 g) nutritional yeast

Salt and pepper, to taste

For the sauté, use the sauté setting over normal, or medium heat, and heat the oil or broth. Add the onion and sauté until transparent, 5 minutes. Then add the garlic, caraway seeds and paprika and sauté for 2 more minutes.

For the pressure cooker, add the water, cabbage, potatoes, carrots, bouillon cube and dill to the onion mixture and stir to combine. Put the lid on and make sure the steam release handle is set to sealing, or closed; change to the manual setting (the pressure cooking one) and set the timer for 5 minutes.

Allow the pressure to release naturally. You'll know when it's ready because the round silver pressure gauge will drop down.

Before serving, mix in the nutritional yeast and add salt and pepper to taste.

PER SERVING: Calories 175.2, protein 8.3 g, total fat 2.8 g, carbohydrates 31.1 g, sodium 56.5 mg, fiber 7.7 g

One of my testers added sauerkraut to his leftovers and loved it. Give it a try if you're a sauerkraut fan, too.

QUICK RED CURRY ZUCCHINI NOODLE SOUP

gluten-free, soy-free, no added oil

Sometimes you need a bowl of steaming soup that has some attitude. This rich, spicy broth is full of veggies. In fact, even the noodles are spiralized zucchini.

MAKES 2 SERVINGS

1½ cups (355 ml) water

¾ cup (175 ml) full-fat coconut milk

1½ tsp (4 g) red curry paste

2" (5-cm) piece lemongrass, smashed (or 1 tsp lemon zest)

1 medium zucchini, spiralized (about 3 cups [360 g])

½ cup (75 g) chopped red pepper

½ cup (64 g) thin carrot coins

2 tbsp (10 g) nutritional yeast

Salt, to taste

FOR SERVING

Lime wedges

Bean sprouts

Chopped cilantro

Add the water, coconut milk, red curry paste, lemongrass, zucchini, red pepper and carrot coins to the Instant Pot.

Put on the lid and close the pressure valve. Click the manual button and set to 1 minute, then click the adjust button and set the pressure to low.

Release the pressure manually, by carefully moving the valve. Stir in the nutritional yeast and salt to taste.

To serve, garnish with the lime wedges, bean sprouts and cilantro.

PER SERVING: Calories 250.8, protein 6.5 g, total fat 16.0 g, carbohydrates 22.8 g, sodium 285.9 mg, fiber 6.4 g

This would work with spiralized sweet potato, carrot, cabbage or butternut squash. That way you can make it with seasonal vegetables all year long!

Technically, this recipe has no added refined oil, but we all know that coconut milk is high in fat. If you are on a no- or restricted-oil diet, you can always use unsweetened coconut milk from a carton, such as So Delicious, and a little coconut extract to get a similar flavor with fewer calories.

MUSHROOM STROGANOFF

gluten-free, soy-free, no added oil option*

I love this creamy mushroom sauce. It's flavored with paprika and dill and turns plain pasta into a soul-soothing meal. My favorite way to serve it is over mashed potatoes when the weather dips below freezing. You can toss a few tablespoons of cashews in with the cauliflower florets to make the sauce creamier, but I think it's great either way.

MAKES 4 SERVINGS

SAUTÉ INGREDIENTS

1 tbsp (15 ml) mild oil (or *dry sauté or add a little water/vegetable broth)

1 cup (160 g) minced onion

1½ tsp (4 g) minced garlic

2 tsp (5 g) paprika

PRESSURE COOKER INGREDIENTS

2 lb (906 g) mushrooms, sliced

½ cup (120 ml) water

1 vegetable bouillon cube

1½ tsp (1.5 g) dried dill

2 cups (248 g) cauliflower florets, wrapped in foil

SAUCE INGREDIENTS

½ cup (120 ml) unsweetened nondairy milk

1 tbsp (5 g) nutritional yeast

½ tsp dill

Salt and pepper, to taste

Cooked gluten-free pasta or mashed potatoes, to serve

For the sauté, use the sauté setting over normal, or medium heat, and heat the oil or broth. Add the onion and sauté until transparent, 5 minutes. Then add the garlic and paprika and sauté for 2 more minutes.

For the pressure cooker, add the mushrooms, water, bouillon cube and dill to the onion mixture and stir to combine. Top with the cauliflower foil packet. Put the lid on and make sure the steam release handle is set to sealing, or closed; change to the manual setting (the pressure cooking one) and set the timer for 10 minutes.

Carefully move the pressure valve to steam release handle and release the pressure manually.

For the sauce, transfer the cooked cauliflower to your blender along with the nondairy milk, nutritional yeast and dill. Blend until smooth and season with salt and pepper to taste. Pour the sauce into the Instant Pot and mix with the mushrooms.

Serve over cooked pasta or mashed potatoes.

PER SERVING: Calories 172.7, protein 10.1 g, total fat 8.4 g, carbohydrates 18.3 g, sodium 49.3 mg, fiber 5.8 g

If you want a little more tang, go ahead and add ½–1 teaspoon lemon juice to the sauce.

LOTS O' VEGGIES BOLOGNESE

gluten-free, soy-free, no added oil

This Bolognese has zero percent meat (of course), but it's full of hearty texture courtesy of all the shredded vegetables. The mushrooms add lots of umami and you'll be surprised just how many veggies you can get into vegetable haters with this sauce!

MAKES 8 SERVINGS

½ head cauliflower, cut into rough florets

1 (10-oz [300-g]) container mushrooms

2 cups (220 g) shredded carrot

2 cups (164 g) eggplant chunks

2 (28-oz [794-g]) cans crushed tomatoes

1 cup (237 ml) water

6 cloves garlic, minced

2 tbsp (32 g) tomato paste

2 tbsp (42 g) agave nectar or sweetener of your choice

2 tbsp (32 g) balsamic vinegar

1½ tbsp (4.5 g) dried oregano

1 tbsp (2 g) dried basil

1½ tsp (2 g) dried rosemary

Salt and pepper, to taste

Add the cauliflower florets to the food processor and pulse until the pieces are tiny and look like couscous. Scrape out into your Instant Pot liner.

Now add the mushrooms to the food processor and pulse until small, then add them to your Instant Pot liner. Repeat with the carrots and eggplant, until all the veggies are minced and in your Instant Pot liner.

Mix in the crushed tomatoes, water, garlic, tomato paste, agave nectar, balsamic vinegar, oregano, basil and rosemary.

Cook on manual with high pressure for 7 minutes and let the pressure release naturally.

Add salt and pepper to taste, and add more oregano, basil or rosemary if you feel that the flavor faded some during cooking. I almost always add a little extra boost with the Italian Spice Blend on page 59.

PER SERVING: Calories 123.8, protein 6.0 g, total fat 1.0 g, carbohydrates 28.0 g, sodium 327.3 mg, fiber 7.0 g

VEGAN CAULIFLOWER QUESO

Cauliflower is a magical vegetable. It's tasty on its own, but it can transform into oil-free creamy sauces and even replace meat. In this recipe, it's the base for my favorite creamy, cheesy queso sauce. This is great on chips but even better on top of burritos and enchiladas. Best of all, you can get the pickiest of eaters to eat their veggies this way.

MAKES 4 CUPS (940 ML)

INSTANT POT INGREDIENTS

2 cups (214 g) cauliflower florets (about ½ head small cauliflower)

1 cup (237 ml) water

¾ cup (96 g) thick-cut carrot coins

¼ cup (34 g) raw cashews

BLENDER INGREDIENTS

¼ cup (24 g) nutritional yeast

Liquid drained from 1 (10-oz [283-g]) can diced tomatoes with green chiles (I like Rotel)

½ tsp smoked paprika

½ tsp salt (or to taste)

¼ tsp chili powder

¼ tsp jalapeño powder (page 56), optional

⅛ tsp mustard powder

MIX-IN INGREDIENTS

1 (10-oz [283-g]) can diced tomatoes with green chiles, drained (I like Rotel)

½ cup (75 g) chopped bell pepper (optional)

2 tbsp (30 g) minced red onion (optional)

¼ cup (4 g) minced cilantro

For the Instant Pot, add the cauliflower, water, carrots and cashews to your Instant Pot and cook on high pressure for 5 minutes, then carefully do a quick pressure release by moving the valve to release the pressure.

Pour the cooked mixture into a strainer over the sink and drain the extra water.

For the blender, put the drained mixture along with the nutritional yeast, liquid drained from the canned tomatoes, smoked paprika, salt, chili powder, jalapeño powder (if using) and mustard powder into your blender. Blend until smooth.

For the mix-ins, scrape out the blender contents into a mixing bowl and stir in the tomatoes and green chiles, bell pepper (if using), minced onion (if using) and cilantro.

You can serve this at room temperature or keep it warm on the lowest slow cooker setting.

PER 1-CUP (240-ML) SERVING: Calories 107.7, protein 6.5 g, total fat 4.2 g, carbohydrates 12.7 g, sodium 162.6 mg, fiber 3.9 g

ASIAN STEAMED DUMPLINGS

gluten-free, soy-free, no added oil option*

Dim sum can be hard to find once you go vegan, but not if you make your own. With store-bought wrappers these are amazingly easy and cheap to make. Be aware that some brands contain egg, but you can always find vegan ones at Asian markets. Believe it or not, this filling is so flavorful you won't even need a dipping sauce.

MAKES 12 DUMPLINGS

SAUTÉ INGREDIENTS

1 tbsp (15 ml) oil (or *dry sauté or add a little water/vegetable broth)

1 cup (70 g) minced shiitake mushrooms (or substitute white mushrooms)

1½ cups (105 g) minced cabbage

½ cup (55 g) shredded carrot

2 tbsp (30 ml) soy sauce

1 tbsp (15 ml) rice wine vinegar

1 tsp grated fresh ginger

1 tsp sesame oil (optional)

12 round vegan dumpling wrappers

For the sauté, use the sauté setting over normal, or do the sauté in a pan on the stove over medium heat. Heat the oil or broth and add the mushrooms once hot. Sauté until the mushrooms release their juices, then add the cabbage, carrot, soy sauce and rice wine vinegar and sauté until the mixture is dry.

Remove the liner from the Instant Pot and set on the stove or a pot holder. Mix in the ginger and sesame oil (if using).

Cut out a round piece of parchment paper to fit inside a 6- or 8-inch (15-or 20-cm) bamboo steamer. You will be able to fit all 12 dumplings in one level of the 8-inch (20-cm) one. No bamboo steamer? Just use your vegetable steamer lightly coated with oil inside your Instant Pot instead.

Get a small bowl of water and set it up next to a cutting board to work on.

Place a wrapper on the cutting board and spread water around the edge with your fingertip. Add 1 tablespoon (15 g) filling to the middle of the wrapper and fold in half, matching the edges. Press together. You can stop here or you can grab it by the middle of the sealed part and fold the dough in two places on either side. Then place in the steamer with the pleated side up.

Put the top on your bamboo steamer (if using) and add 1½ cups (355 ml) water and your rack to your Instant Pot. Then lower the steamer into the pot.

Put the lid on and make sure that the steam release handle is sealed. Select the steam setting and lower the time to 7 minutes.

Open the steam release valve manually.

PER DUMPLING: Calories 30.8, protein 0.5 g, total fat 1.6 g, carbohydrates 1.6 g, sodium 156.6 mg, fiber 0.5 g

Another way a tester did it was with two Instant Pot racks. You can get a cheap extra rack on Amazon or at an Asian market (see "Accessory Resources," page 209). She put 10 dumplings on a parchment-covered Instant Pot rack, flipped the other Instant Pot rack upside down, covered it with parchment and placed another 10 dumplings on it.

If you are using an 8-inch (20-cm) bamboo steamer you can fill up both layers and make a double batch of dumplings. Your lid may not fit, but it's okay to leave it off.

MUSHROOM POTATO TACO FILLING

gluten-free, soy-free, no added oil

Ever since my trip to Mexico last year, I have been in love with Mexican food. Mushrooms were a default vegetarian substitute, and for good reason. Their umami flavor really works well. This filling also has potatoes and is great over quinoa or wrapped in your favorite tortilla.

MAKES 8 TACOS

8 oz (224 g) mushrooms, sliced

½ cup (75 g) minced poblano pepper (or substitute bell pepper)

4 cloves garlic, minced (about 1½ tsp [4 g])

1 tsp ground cumin

1 tsp smoked paprika

½ tsp chili powder (or more if you like it spicy)

½ cup (120 ml) water

2 cups (300 g) diced potato

Salt, to taste

TO SERVE

Taco shells

Shredded lettuce

Cashew cream

Chopped cilantro

Diced tomatoes

Using the sauté setting over normal, or medium heat, sauté the mushrooms, pepper and garlic until the mushrooms begin to release their juices. If the mushroom slices are large, go ahead and chop them up with your spatula while you are cooking them.

Next add the cumin, smoked paprika and chili powder and sauté about 1 minute more, or until the spices become fragrant. Pour in the water and stir to combine.

Add the potatoes and press them under the water. Put the lid on and make sure the steam release handle is set to sealing, or closed; cook on high pressure for 10 minutes.

Carefully move the pressure valve to steam release handle and let the pressure release manually. Add salt to taste.

If the mixture is a little on the thin side, mash a few of the potato pieces and mix well. You can also turn the sauté function back on and cook until the water reduces to where you'd like it.

Serve in your favorite soft or hard taco shells topped with shredded lettuce, cashew cream, chopped cilantro and fresh diced tomatoes.

PER SERVING: Calories 36.8, protein 1.7 g, total fat 0.1 g, carbohydrates 7.9 g, sodium 7.3 mg, fiber 1.4 g

SPICY JACKFRUIT TINGA

gluten-free, soy-free, no added oil option*

This flavorful Mexican dish uses jackfruit. Be sure to use canned young jackfruit in brine. Fresh or sweetened will not work. If you can't get the correct form of jackfruit where you live, you can substitute shredded sweet potato or butternut squash.

MAKES 4 SERVINGS

SAUTÉ INGREDIENTS

1 tbsp (15 ml) mild oil (or *dry sauté or add a little water/vegetable broth)

1½ cups (240 g) minced onion

6 cloves garlic, minced

2 tbsp (11 g) minced jalapeño

PRESSURE COOKER INGREDIENTS

1 (20-oz [565-g]) can jackfruit in brine, rinsed

1 (14.5-oz [411-g]) can diced tomatoes

1 cup (132 g) diced tomatillos

¼ cup (60 ml) water

1½ tsp (1.5 g) dried thyme

1 tsp dried oregano

½ tsp ground cumin

1 chipotle in adobo sauce, minced (optional)

Salt, to taste

Tortillas or your favorite cooked grain, to serve

For the sauté, use the sauté setting over normal, or medium heat, and heat the oil or broth. Add the onion and sauté until transparent, 5 minutes. Then add the garlic and jalapeño and sauté for 1 minute more.

For the pressure cooker, rinse the jackfruit in a strainer then smash it in your hands to get it to break into shreds. You can remove any large seedpods and discard. They will be obvious once you start smashing. Add the jackfruit, tomatoes, tomatillos, water, thyme, oregano, cumin and chipotle (if using) to the onion mixture and stir to combine.

Put the lid on and make sure the steam release handle is set to sealing, or closed; change to the manual setting (the pressure cooking one) and set the timer for 15 minutes. Allow the pressure to release naturally.

If there's still too much liquid, turn on the sauté function again and cook until it thickens. Adjust the seasonings and add salt to taste. Serve in a tortilla or over your favorite grain.

PER SERVING: Calories 123.7, protein 3.2 g, total fat 4.3 g, carbohydrates 20.6 g, sodium 647.8 mg, fiber 6.0 g

CHAPTER 6

Fast and Comforting One-Pot Meals

One-pot meals are a reason to buy an Instant Pot, if nothing else has swayed you yet. Soups, stews and even pasta can be made in a snap—all with only one pot to clean after dinner. You can skip expensive dim sum and steam your own buns right in your very own Instant Pot!

While some of the recipes have been divided up by beans, grains and vegetables, this chapter is more of a mix and match one.

MUSHROOM AND BUTTERNUT SQUASH CHILI BEAN SOUP

gluten-free, soy-free, no added oil

This has all the great flavors of chili with the added sweetness of butternut squash and rich umami flavor from mushrooms. It's filling enough to be dinner, but elegant enough to serve as a starter to a dress-up meal.

MAKES 6 SERVINGS

PRESSURE COOKER INGREDIENTS

3 cups (700 ml) water

1 lb (454 g) mushrooms, chopped

2 cups (410 g) diced butternut squash

½ lb (225 g) dried kidney or black beans, soaked for at least 8 hours and drained

2 tsp (6 g) minced garlic

1½ tsp (4 g) chili powder

1½ tsp (4 g) cumin powder

1½ tsp (1.5 g) dried thyme

1½ tsp (1.5 g) dried oregano

SAUTÉ INGREDIENTS

1 cup (250 g) tomato puree or crushed tomatoes

½ cup (48 g) nutritional yeast

1 tsp apple cider vinegar

1 tsp smoked paprika

½ tsp liquid smoke

Salt and pepper, to taste

TO SERVE

Cauliflower Sour Cream (page 40)

Cashew cream

Salsa

For the pressure cooker, add the water, mushrooms, squash, beans, garlic, chili powder, cumin, thyme and oregano to your Instant Pot. Put the lid on and make sure the steam release handle is closed. Select the manual setting and set to cook for 10 minutes. The Instant Pot timer will begin counting down the time once it gets up to pressure.

Allow the pressure to release naturally.

For the sauté, remove the lid and add the tomatoes, nutritional yeast, apple cider vinegar, paprika and liquid smoke to the squash mixture and stir to combine. Leave the lid off, change to the sauté function and cook until the soup is thoroughly heated and the flavor of the tomatoes have tamed a bit, about 10 minutes.

Add salt and pepper to taste and serve topped with Cauliflower Sour Cream, cashew cream or salsa.

PER SERVING: Calories 111.3, protein 7.9 g, total fat 0.8 g, carbohydrates 22.4 g, sodium 208.0 mg, fiber 7.5 g

MIX AND MATCH MISO SOUP

gluten-free, soy-free option*, no added oil option**

The Japanese are smart and eat this as a nutritious start to their day. I say it's great anytime of the day. It's warming and filling, and there's something about eating miso that makes me feel balanced and ready to tackle anything.

MAKES 4 SERVINGS

SAUTÉ INGREDIENTS

1 tbsp (15 ml) oil (or **dry sauté or add a little water/vegetable broth)

¼ cup (40 g) minced onion

2 cloves garlic, minced

PRESSURE COOKER INGREDIENTS

4 cups (940 ml) water

1 medium carrot, cut into half-moons

BEFORE SERVING

½ (14-oz [397-g]) package firm tofu, pressed and cubed (or *use hemp tofu)

½ cup (35 g) shredded cabbage or 2 baby bok choy, quartered

3 tbsp (52 g) red miso (or your favorite miso) (or *use chickpea miso)

2 tbsp (10 g) nutritional yeast

EXTRAS

Chopped scallion

Sesame oil

Sriracha

Bean sprouts

For the sauté, use the sauté setting over normal, or medium heat, and heat the oil or broth. Add the onion and sauté until transparent, 5 minutes. Then add the garlic and sauté for 2 more minutes.

For the pressure cooker, add the water and carrot to the onion mixture and stir to combine. Put the lid on and make sure the steam release handle is set to sealing, or closed; cook on high pressure for 5 minutes.

Release the pressure manually by carefully opening the valve. Remove the lid and change the setting back to sauté.

Before serving, add in the tofu and cabbage and heat until warm, about 5 minutes. Whisk in the miso and nutritional yeast.

Ladle out and top with any of the extras you'd like.

PER SERVING: Calories 87.7, protein 5.4 g, total fat 5.4 g, carbohydrates 5.5 g, sodium 47.3 mg, fiber 1.7 g

BECKY STRIEPE'S BROWN RICE CONGEE WITH SALT AND PEPPER TOFU

gluten-free, soy-free option*, no added oil

Becky Striepe is the blogger behind GlueAndGlitter.com and develops some amazing recipes. She's letting me share her comforting whole-grain congee recipe with you. It's great if you have an upset tummy or just a hard week.

MAKES 4 SERVINGS

PRESSURE COOKER INGREDIENTS

½ cup (93 g) long-grain brown rice

4 cups (940 ml) mushroom broth, homemade (page 47) or store-bought

2 cups (140 g) chopped bok choy (green and white parts)

2 cups (194 g) halved shiitake mushrooms (or substitute baby bella mushrooms)

2 cloves garlic, minced

2 tbsp (12 g) minced ginger

SERVING INGREDIENTS

1 recipe Salt and Pepper Tofu (recipe follows)

2 scallions, diced

Soy sauce, to taste

For the pressure cooker, add the rice, broth, bok choy, mushrooms, garlic and ginger to your Instant Pot. Put the lid on and make sure the steam release handle is sealed. Cook on manual setting at high pressure for 40 minutes. Let the pressure release naturally.

To serve, spoon into bowls and top with the tofu and scallions. Add soy sauce to taste.

PER SERVING: Calories 108.4, protein 9.6 g, total fat 3.8 g, carbohydrates 11.7 g, sodium 567.1 mg, fiber 1.9 g

SALT AND PEPPER TOFU

1 (1-lb [454-g]) block tofu, sliced into small squares (or *use hemp tofu or roasted cauliflower florets)

Salt and black pepper, to taste

Preheat the oven to 425°F (220°C, or gas mark 7). Arrange the sliced tofu on a baking sheet lined with a parchment paper. Sprinkle salt and pepper over the tofu, bake for 20 minutes, and then flip the pieces over.

Sprinkle salt and pepper over the other side of the tofu, and bake for 10 more minutes.

SUMMER CONGEE

gluten-free option*, soy-free option**, no added oil

This congee is perfect for a summer cold or any time you might be feeling weak or under the weather.
It has nourishing whole grains, moong dal, vegetables and other healing ingredients.

MAKES 4 SERVINGS

6 cups (1.4 L) vegetable broth (or water with 1 bouillon cube)

1 cup (164 g) corn kernels

1 cup (110 g) grated carrot

½ cup (51 g) minced celery

⅓ cup (41 g) moong dal (or substitute adzuki beans)

⅓ cup (39 g) millet

⅓ cup (61 g) brown rice

1 tbsp (15 ml) soy sauce (or *soy sauce clearly labeled gluten-free for gluten-free option or **coconut aminos for a soy-free version)

2 tsp (4 g) grated ginger

½ tsp ground ginger

½ tsp ground turmeric

½ tsp salt

¼ tsp black pepper

TOPPING CHOICES
Chopped scallions

Chopped cilantro

Sliced hot pepper

Sesame oil

Extra grated fresh ginger

Extra soy sauce

Place the broth, corn, carrot, celery, moong dal, millet, brown rice, soy sauce, grated and ground ginger, turmeric, salt and pepper into your Instant Pot. Put on the lid and set the steam release handle to sealing. Click the porridge button, then click the adjust button once to make the time change to 30 minutes. Let the pressure release naturally.

Serve with bowls of your choice of toppings to make your congee just the way you like it.

PER SERVING: Calories 124.8, protein 3.9 g, total fat 0.8 g, carbohydrates 22.6 g, sodium 1673.8 mg, fiber 2.6 g

EASY ANDOUILLE JAMBALAYA

gluten-free option*, soy-free option**, no added oil option***

This is my very favorite one-pot meal. It has it all—whole grains, protein, vegetables and lots of big flavors. It also is a great dish to bring to potlucks or have for an inexpensive dinner party.

MAKES 6 SERVINGS

SAUTÉ INGREDIENTS

1 tbsp (15 ml) mild oil (or ***dry sauté or add a little water/vegetable broth)

1½ cups (240 g) minced onion

4 cloves garlic, minced

2 cups (300 g) chopped bell pepper

1 cup (101 g) chopped celery

2 tbsp (11 g) Cajun Spice Blend (page 60)

PRESSURE COOKER INGREDIENTS

2 cups (280 g) chopped vegan andouille links (about 4 large) (or *use tofu, tempeh, cauliflower florets or chickpeas to make gluten-free or **use the soy-free recipe on page 52)

2¼ cups (535 ml) water

2 cups (370 g) long-grain brown rice

1 (14.5-oz [411-g]) can diced or crushed tomatoes (or 1½ cups [270 g] fresh)

Salt and pepper, to taste

Hot sauce, to serve

For the sauté, use the sauté setting over normal, or medium heat, and heat the oil or broth. Add the onion and sauté until transparent, 5 minutes. Then add the garlic, bell pepper, celery and Cajun Spice Blend and sauté for a minute more.

For the pressure cooker, add the andouille, water, rice and tomatoes to the onion mixture and stir to combine. Put the lid on and make sure that the steam release handle is sealed. Cook on manual setting at high pressure and set for 30 minutes. Let the pressure release naturally.

Season with salt and pepper. Serve with lots of hot sauce on the side. I love garlic Tabasco, but you can use any hot sauce that you like.

PER SERVING: Calories 200.8, protein 15.9 g, total fat 3.5 g, carbohydrates 27.8 g, sodium 31.5 mg, fiber 3.8 g

NURTURE YOURSELF NAVY BEAN SORGHUM STEW

gluten-free, soy-free, no added oil

If you're feeling exhausted, a little let down or even just plain sick, this is the stew for you. It's ridiculously easy to make and you can take a nap while it's cooking. It has a delicate flavor and is gentle on your stomach. This was the first recipe in which I ever used sorghum, but you could use Kamut, spelt, wheat berries, oat groats or any long-cooking grain.

MAKES 6 SERVINGS

PRESSURE COOKER INGREDIENTS

6 cups (1.4 L) water

2 vegan bouillon cubes

2 cups (256 g) shredded or chopped carrot

1 cup (208 g) dried navy beans

1 cup (192 g) dried sorghum grain (not flour)

BEFORE SERVING

2 cups (32 g) minced kale or collard greens

½ cup (48 g) nutritional yeast

Salt and pepper, to taste

For the pressure cooker, add the water, bouillon, carrot, navy beans and sorghum to your Instant Pot and mix together.

Put on the lid and set to sealing, or close the steam release handle. Click the multigrain button, then click the adjust button 1 time. This will show 60 minutes on the display, but it's actually a special setting. It will soak everything in warm water for 40 minutes before it starts bringing it up to high pressure to cook for 60 minutes.

Let the pressure release naturally.

Before serving, stir in the kale and nutritional yeast. Depending on the bouillon you may want to add salt and pepper as well.

PER SERVING: Calories 220.6, protein 12.0 g, total fat 2.2 g, carbohydrates 41.4 g, sodium 601.3 mg, fiber 6.7 g

You can dress this up with one of the spice blends if you'd like, but I find that with bouillon and the broth from the beans and sorghum it is flavored to my liking.

JL FIELDS'S ONE-POT BLACK-EYED PEAS AND RICE

gluten-free, soy-free, no added oil option*

You may know JL from her book, *Vegan Pressure Cooking*, or from her site, JLgoesVegan.com. She's a dynamic vegan educator and coach, as well as a recipe developer who understands what cooking in the real world means. This simple black-eyed pea recipe adds grain, veggies and a punch of flavor into a quick weeknight meal, which is JL's specialty.

MAKES 4 SERVINGS

SAUTÉ INGREDIENTS

1 tsp extra virgin olive oil (or *dry sauté or add a little water/vegetable broth)

1 large onion, diced

2 carrots, diced

3 celery stalks, diced

3 cloves garlic, minced

PRESSURE COOKER INGREDIENTS

1 medium tomato, diced

1 cup (145 g) dried black-eyed peas

½ cup (93 g) white rice

1 tsp dried parsley

1 tsp dried oregano

1 tsp crushed red pepper

¼ tsp ground black pepper

¼ tsp ground cumin

¼ cup (66 g) tomato paste

2½ cups (570 ml) vegetable broth (or water with bouillon)

BEFORE SERVING INGREDIENTS

2 tbsp (30 ml) lemon juice, or to taste

Salt, to taste

For the sauté, use the sauté setting over normal, or medium heat, and heat the oil or broth. Add the onion, carrots, celery and garlic and sauté for 5–8 minutes, until the vegetables are soft.

For the pressure cooker, add the tomato, black-eyed peas, rice, spices, tomato paste and broth to the onion mixture and stir to combine. Put the lid on and make sure that the vent is sealed. Cook on manual setting at high pressure and set for 8 minutes.

Let the pressure release naturally. If there's too much liquid, switch back to the sauté setting and heat until the extra liquid evaporates.

Before serving, stir in the lemon juice and add salt to taste.

PER SERVING: Calories 140.3, protein 3.8 g, total fat 1.7 g, carbohydrates 28.5 g, sodium 785.3 mg, fiber 5.3 g

Prefer not to use white rice? Try a combination of millet and quinoa in its place. Use the same amount and cook for the same time. *Voilà!* A whole-grain version in the same amount of time.

You can also change out the black-eyed peas for lentils or moong dal if that's what you have on hand. They all require the same cooking times.

WELCOME SPRING PEA AND ASPARAGUS RISOTTO

gluten-free, soy-free, no added oil

Sometimes winter seems to last forever. That all changes as soon as the asparagus starts to peek out. It's about the time I start adding some pea tendrils into our salads. This risotto truly celebrates my favorite point in time. If you'd prefer a whole-grain version, try substituting quinoa because it will use the same cooking time.

MAKES 4 SERVINGS

4 cups (940 ml) water, divided

1½ cups (279 g) Arborio rice

1 tbsp (8 g) or 1 cube vegetable bouillon

1½ cups (201 g) chopped asparagus (if thick cut into ½" [1.3-cm] pieces, if thin cut into 1" [2.5-cm] pieces)

1 cup (134 g) fresh or frozen sweet green peas

2 tbsp (10 g) nutritional yeast

1 tbsp (15 ml) lemon juice

Salt and pepper, to taste

Fresh chopped thyme or tarragon, for garnish

Add 3½ cups (820 ml) of the water, the rice and the bouillon to your Instant Pot. Put the lid on and close the pressure release valve.

Cook on high pressure for 5 minutes. Carefully open the pressure release valve to bring the pressure down manually.

Stir in the remaining ½ cup (120 ml) water, the asparagus, peas, nutritional yeast and lemon juice. Turn on the sauté function and set to low. Cook until the asparagus and peas are tender, about 5 minutes. If it cooks dry, you can add extra water as needed.

Before serving, season to taste with salt and pepper. Top with fresh chopped herbs.

PER SERVING: Calories 305.0, protein 9.7 g, total fat 0.6 g, carbohydrates 64.1 g, sodium 501.0 mg, fiber 4.8 g

Use this recipe as a base for the bounty in other seasons as well.
Fall—Add in butternut squash cubes and cook with the rice. Season with garam masala and garnish with chopped kale.
Winter—Sauté some onions and mushrooms, then add the rice and cook. Season with rosemary and sage.
Summer—Use chopped summer squash, chopped green beans and fresh tomato instead of the spring veggies called for.

WINTER ONE-POT LENTILS AND RICE

gluten-free, soy-free, no oil added option*

Some nights are so cold it's hard to tear yourself away from the fire to make dinner. This is the recipe you need to make. It's hearty and filling, and uses staples from your pantry. Plus, there's only about 10 minutes of hands-on time, then you can go back to the couch and curl up under a throw until it's ready to eat.

MAKES 4 SERVINGS

SAUTÉ INGREDIENTS

1 tbsp (15 ml) oil (or *dry sauté or add a little water/vegetable broth)

½ cup (80 g) chopped onion

2 cloves garlic, minced

PRESSURE COOKER INGREDIENTS

3½ cups (820 ml) water

1½ cups (278 g) brown rice

1 cup (192 g) brown lentils

1 cup (160 g) peeled and diced rutabaga (or turnip or potato)

2" (5-cm) sprig fresh rosemary

1 tbsp (2 g) dried marjoram (or thyme)

Salt and pepper, to taste

For the sauté, use the sauté setting over normal, or medium heat, and heat the oil or broth. Add the onion and sauté until transparent, 5 minutes. Then add the garlic and sauté a minute more.

For the pressure cooker, add the water, brown rice, lentils, rutabaga, rosemary and marjoram to the onion mixture and stir to combine. Put the lid on and make sure that the vent is sealed. Cook on manual setting at high pressure and set for 23 minutes.

Let the pressure release naturally. Season with salt and pepper before serving and add more marjoram and ground rosemary as needed.

PER SERVING: Calories 188.5, protein 7.0 g, total fat 4.4 g, carbohydrates 31.1 g, sodium 27.3 mg, fiber 6.2 g

BBQ WHOLE-GRAIN STEAMED BUNS

gluten-free*, soy-free, no added oil

These are so much fun to make. I'd suggest getting a few friends together and make a day of it.
First you make the whole-grain dough, then make the filling and stuff them. Freeze some for next time
and steam the rest to eat right now! You can double or triple the recipe easily.

MAKES 12 BUNS

DOUGH INGREDIENTS

1¼ cups (290 ml) warm water

1 tbsp (20 g) agave nectar or maple
syrup

1 tbsp (18 g) active dry yeast

2 cups (272 g) whole wheat flour

1 cup (136 g) spelt flour (or whole
wheat)

½ tsp salt

FILLING INGREDIENTS

2 cups (454 g) dry soy curls, broken
into small pieces

3 cups (700 ml) boiling water

3 tbsp (48 g) hoisin sauce

2 tbsp (12 g) grated ginger

2 tsp (10 ml) Sriracha (add more if you
want it spicy)

2 tsp (10 ml) soy sauce

½ tsp seasoned rice vinegar

There are so many variations
you can do with this. Use Gardein
or Beyond Meat in place of the
soy curls or use cooked millet
and quinoa instead of a meat
substitute.

For the dough, mix the warm water with the agave and yeast in your mixer bowl.
Let sit for about 10 minutes, or until the mixture begins to foam. This lets you know
the yeast is fresh and ready to get to work!

In a separate mixing bowl, combine the flours and salt. Add the flour mixture to
the mixer bowl with the yeast. Using your dough hook, mix for about 8 minutes. In
between you may need to stop and scrape the flour from the sides with a spatula
to get it all to incorporate.

No mixer or dough hook? You can mix the ingredients by hand in a large mixing
bowl. Then lightly flour a cutting board and knead the dough by hand until it's
elastic and feels like your earlobe.

Roll the dough into a large ball, cover with a clean dish towel and let sit in a warm
place to rise. The dough is ready to be used when you poke your finger in the
dough and the indention remains. The dough will double in size by this time as well.

For the filling, place the soy curls in a heatproof bowl and pour the boiling water
over. It will take about 10 minutes for them to reconstitute.

While you're waiting, in a mixing bowl, whisk together the hoisin sauce, ginger,
Sriracha, soy sauce and rice vinegar. Squeeze the water out of the soy curls and
add to the sauce mixture.

Cover the bottom of an 8-inch (20-cm) bamboo steamer with parchment paper.

Divide the dough into 12 equal balls. Using the palm of your hand or a rolling pin, press
them into circles 3 to 4 inches (7.5 to 10 cm) in diameter. Do not make them paper-
thin or they will tear and your filling will fall out. I promise you, this will make you sad.
Add a heaping teaspoon of the soy curl filling to the middle of the dough circle
and gather up the edges. You can do fancy finishes on the buns, but if these are
your first just make it look like a round roll on top and put the gathered side on the
bottom in the steamer. Repeat until all the buns are ready to be steamed.

Set a rack in your Instant Pot and add 1½ cups (355 ml) water. The water should just
come up to the bottom of the rack. Lower the steamer onto the rack with its lid on.
Use the steam setting and set the time to 10 minutes.

PER BUN: Calories 125.6, protein 6.0 g, total fat 1.7 g, carbohydrates 24.0 g, sodium
192.7 mg, fiber 3.7 g

MINI TOFU FRITTATAS

This is a little breakfast dish that you can whip up fast and use up those little bits of veggies you have stashed in the fridge. Serve for brunch with a green salad and some juice. You'll need four large ramekins, about 4 inches (10 cm) wide.

MAKES 4 SERVINGS

SAUTÉ INGREDIENTS

1 tbsp (15 ml) oil (or *dry sauté or add a little water/vegetable broth)

½ cup (80 g) minced onion

½ cup (35 g) minced mushrooms

⅓ cup (49 g) minced bell pepper

⅓ cup (36 g) grated carrot

⅓ cup (30 g) minced kale, collards or spinach

TOFU MIXTURE INGREDIENTS

1 (14-oz [397-g]) package firm tofu, quickly pressed to remove most of the liquid (if you remove all the liquid by pressing overnight it won't blend well)

2 tbsp (10 g) nutritional yeast

1½ tsp (4 g) kala namak or black salt

2 tsp (2 g) herbs de Provence or Italian blend

½ tsp ground turmeric

Salt and pepper, to taste

For the sauté, use the sauté setting over normal, or do the sauté in a pan on the stove over medium heat. Heat the oil or broth, add the onion and sauté until translucent, 5 minutes. Add the mushrooms and cook until they release their juices, then add the bell pepper and carrot, and sauté until the mixture is dry. Stir in the kale and set aside to cool.

For the tofu mixture, add the tofu, nutritional yeast, kala namak, herbs and turmeric to your blender. Blend until silky smooth. You can add a few tablespoons (30–45 ml) of water if you need to, but you should be able to scrape down a few times to get everything blended together.

Combine the cooled veggies and tofu mixture in a bowl with a pour spout. Add salt and pepper to taste.

Oil four 4-inch (10-cm) ramekins and divide the mixture among them. Cover each one with foil.

Place the rack in your Instant Pot and add 1½ cups (355 ml) water. Carefully sit 2 of the ramekins in catty-cornered, then balance the other 2 on top of those.

Place the lid on and seal the valve. Cook on high pressure for 15 minutes and allow a natural pressure release.

You will need to carefully remove the ramekins because they will be very hot. You can use tongs or mini pot holders to remove them without burning yourself.

PER SERVING: Calories 130.3, protein 10.5 g, total fat 7.8 g, carbohydrates 7.0 g, sodium 22.7 mg, fiber 2.5 g

I sauté the first part of this on the stove top because I prefer to start with a clean insert for cooking the frittatas once they are assembled. You can sauté in the insert, then wash and dry it before cooking the frittatas if you don't have access to a stove.

RICOTTA PENNE PIE

gluten-free option*, soy-free, no added oil option**

If you use a 7-inch (17.5-cm) springform pan or an 8-inch (20-cm) cake pan with a removable bottom this is a show-stopper. It's like bringing a pasta cake out to the dinner table. If you don't want to bother with all that, just make it in a round casserole or soufflé pan that fits in your Instant Pot. Either way, it's a quick, mostly hands-off dinner.

MAKES 8 SERVINGS

3½ cups (924 g) pasta sauce, homemade (page 51) or store-bought

3 cups (192 g) *brown rice or whole wheat penne pasta

1 cup (248 g) vegan ricotta, homemade (page 39) or store-bought

2 tbsp (14 g) ground flaxseed

Mix everything together in a large bowl. Oil a 7-inch (17.5-cm) springform pan or an 8-inch (20-cm) cake pan. If you use a springform or cake pan with a removable bottom, before you add the mixture be sure to cover the underside of the pan with foil, so no sauce seeps through.

Add the rack to your Instant Pot and pour in 1½ cups (355 ml) water.

Spread the pasta mixture in the pan and cover with foil. If your pan does not fit inside the rack handles, you will need to fashion some handles out of aluminum foil to lower the pan into the cooker. Tear off two pieces of foil about 3 feet (1 m) long, fold each one lengthwise two times. Lay the foil handles out on the counter in a plus sign near your cooker. Place your pan in the center, where the two pieces cross. Pull the handles up and carefully lift the pan into your Instant Pot.

Cook on high pressure for 20 minutes and let the pressure release naturally.

If you are using a pan with a removable bottom, let sit for 10–15 minutes so that it's cool enough to hold together before you remove it using the foil handles. You can make it easy on yourself and serve it casserole-style instead.

PER SERVING: Calories 261.6, protein 8.8 g, total fat 10.0 g, carbohydrates 37.6 g, sodium 543.4 mg, fiber 4.1 g

Add sautéed mushrooms or cooked vegan Italian sausage crumbles to the pasta mixture to give it a little more flair.

CHAPTER 7

Cook It All At the Same Time: Layered Meals with Sides

The recipes in this chapter were the most fun for me to create. If you have people over to show off what your Instant Pot can do, pulling out different cooking containers, each one containing a piece of a full meal, is the way to do it.

There are wonderful recipes here, such as two Indian curries and rice cooked together, and French lentils and herbs with beets and pink rice, not to mention homemade pierogies.

Many of these recipes can be put together in minutes and the rest of the time is hands off. Now that's a way to throw an easy dinner party!

HERBED FRENCH LENTILS WITH BEETS AND PINK RICE

gluten-free, soy-free, no added oil

If you think you can only make stews, one-pot meals or the ordinary from your Instant Pot, think again. This layered meal is as elegant as it is easy. There's something so classy about those tiny green French lentils, and they look great on top of pink rice surrounded by bright-red cooked beets. This is a perfect dinner party recipe! Be sure to look at "Accessory Resources" on page 209 to find easy ways to cook layered meals.

MAKES 4 SERVINGS

BEET LAYER

2 cups (475 ml) water

3 cups (408 g) peeled and cubed beets
(about 4 medium)

FRENCH LENTIL LAYER

1½ cups (355 ml) water

1 cup (192 g) green French lentils

½ cup (64 g) thinly sliced carrot coins
or 6 baby carrots, split in half

¾ tsp dried thyme

¼ tsp dried tarragon

⅛ tsp ground rosemary

PINK RICE LAYER

1¼ cups (285 ml) water

1 cup (180 g) Madagascar pink rice

For the beet layer, add the 2 cups (475 ml) water and beets to your Instant Pot and spread evenly.

For the French lentil layer, combine the 1½ cups (355 ml) water, lentils, carrots and herbs in a 3-cup (700-ml) Pyrex container, cover with foil and place on the beets.

For the rice layer, mix the 1¼ cups (285 ml) water with the rice in another Pyrex container, cover with foil and place on top of the dish containing the lentils.

Cook on high pressure for 12 minutes. Let the pressure release naturally. Once the pressure indicator goes down, remove the lid and carefully lift out the pans

PER SERVING: Calories 259.4, protein 9.3 g, total fat 1.5 g, carbohydrates 54.6 g, sodium 91.6 mg, fiber 8.7 g

If you have some of Miyoko's amazing cultured vegan cheese, crumble a little on the top of this. It's amazing!

No pink rice? Substitute red rice, jade pearl rice or millet.

Love beets as much as I do? Strain the beet cooking water and mix with 1 cup (200 g) vegan sugar to make beet syrup. Muddle some fresh thyme, add soda water and maybe a splash of gin if you imbibe.

TEMPEH, POTATO AND KALE BOWL

gluten-free, soy-free option*, no added oil

From the first time I made this layered dish, it has become a household favorite. It's great for breakfast, lunch or dinner. The potatoes are slightly smoky, the greens have a garlicky bite and the tempeh has a slightly sweet and spicy tone. All the liquid will not be absorbed by the tempeh, so I suggest giving it a quick pan-fry right before serving.

MAKES 4 SERVINGS

POTATO LAYER

1 (28-oz [794-g]) bag new or baby potatoes, cut into quarters

TEMPEH LAYER

¼ cup (60 ml) water

2 tbsp (30 ml) maple syrup

2 tsp (10 ml) soy sauce

1 tsp Sriracha (or your favorite hot sauce, to taste)

1 (8-oz [255-g]) package tempeh, cut into small cubes (or *use hemp tofu)

KALE LAYER

4 cups (64 g) chopped kale

2 tbsp (10 g) nutritional yeast

1 tbsp (15 ml) water

1 tsp minced garlic

POTATO SEASONING

1 tsp smoked paprika

Salt and pepper, to taste

For the potato layer, add 1½ cups (355 ml) water to your Instant Pot, add a vegetable steamer and spread out the potatoes.

For the tempeh layer, add all the tempeh ingredients to a short Pyrex pan and toss to coat. Cover with foil and place on the potatoes.

For the kale layer, mix the kale, nutritional yeast, water and garlic together in a mixing bowl, transfer to a short Pyrex pan, cover with foil and place on top of the dish containing the tempeh. If you like your tempeh less cooked, wrap in foil, then put in the Pyrex.

Cook on high pressure for 10 minutes. Let the pressure release naturally. Once the pressure indicator goes down, remove the lid and carefully lift out the pans.

For the potato seasoning, toss the potatoes in a large bowl with the paprika, then add salt and pepper to taste.

Serve in a bowl in layers or on a plate. Either way, it's a meal that can't be beat!

PER SERVING: Calories 337.7, protein 19.1 g, total fat 7.9 g, carbohydrates 52.7 g, sodium 245.7 mg, fiber 7.9 g

I use a Pyrex 3-cup (700-ml) small rectangular pan for this. You can fit two on top of the rack included with your Instant Pot and you can even store the leftovers right in the cooking containers! Be sure to take a look at "Accessory Resources" on page 209 for more options.

ONE-POT BURRITO BOWLS

gluten-free, soy-free, no added oil

Bowls are all the rage and I couldn't stop thinking about the layering possibilities in the Instant Pot.
In this recipe we cook quinoa, spicy beans and sweet, smoky onions and peppers, and top it all off with
a warm tomato corn salsa. All I have to say about this one is yum!

MAKES 4 SERVINGS

BEAN LAYER

1 cup (193 g) dried cranberry, pinto or similar beans, soaked overnight, drained

2 cups (475 ml) water

2 tsp (5 g) chili powder

1 tsp minced garlic

½ tsp jalapeño powder

¼ tsp chipotle pepper powder, or to taste

¼ tsp liquid smoke

QUINOA LAYER

1 cup (111 g) quinoa

2 cups (475 ml) water

½ tsp ground cumin

VEGETABLE LAYER

¾ cup (120 g) thinly sliced onion

¾ cup (120 g) thinly sliced bell pepper

¼ tsp smoked paprika

⅛ tsp salt

CORN SALSA LAYER

1 medium tomato, diced (about 1 cup [180 g])

1 cup (164 g) corn kernels

½ cup (75 g) chopped bell pepper

2 tbsp (17 g) minced green chile (from a can; to taste, if using fresh)

Juice from ½ lime (about 2 tbsp [30 ml])

½ tsp salt

OPTIONAL TOPPINGS

Cashew cream

Chopped jalapeños

Your favorite salsa

Hot sauce

Sliced avocado

Shredded carrot

For the bean layer, combine the beans, water and seasonings in your Instant Pot insert.

For the quinoa layer, combine the quinoa, water and cumin in a Pyrex dish. If your pan does not fit inside the rack handles, you will need to fashion some handles out of aluminum foil to lower the pan into the cooker. Tear off two pieces of foil about 3 feet (1 m) long, fold each one lengthwise two times. Lay the foil handles out on the counter in a plus sign near your cooker. Place your pan in the center, where the two pieces cross. Pull the handles up and carefully lift the pan, uncovered, into your Instant Pot, on top of the beans.

For the vegetable layer, combine the onion, pepper, paprika and salt in a bowl, then wrap in a foil packet and place on top of the quinoa container.

For the salsa layer, combine the tomato, corn, bell pepper, green chile, lime juice and salt in a bowl, wrap it in another foil packet and place on top

Cook on high pressure for 12 minutes. Let the pressure release naturally. Once the pressure indicator goes down, remove the lid and lift out the foil packets carefully. Lift out the Pyrex dish using the foil handles.

Serve as a bowl with the quinoa on the bottom topped with the beans, corn salsa, onion and pepper, plus any of the optional toppings that pique your interest.

PER SERVING: Calories 281.4, protein 11.7 g, total fat 3.4 g, carbohydrates 54.2 g, sodium 37.7 mg, fiber 9.3 g

POTATO, VEGETABLE AND TEMPEH GADO-GADO

gluten-free, soy-free option*, no added oil

Gado-gado is a dish that originated in Indonesia, just like tempeh, so I love serving the two of them together. The main thing that ties this recipe together is the thick, rich and slightly spicy coconut peanut sauce that you cook the tempeh in. This is a great dinner party dish. You can even make a buffet with all the toppings and let your guests create their own masterpiece.

MAKES 4 SERVINGS

POTATO LAYER

4 medium potatoes, peeled and cut into chunks

TEMPEH AND SAUCE LAYER

¾ cup (175 ml) full-fat coconut milk

¾ cup (194 g) peanut butter

¼ cup (60 ml) water

2 tbsp (30 ml) soy sauce

1 tbsp (15 ml) rice vinegar or lime juice

1 tbsp (5 g) nutritional yeast

2 tsp (18 g) grated ginger

1 tsp minced garlic

1 tsp Sriracha (or more if you'd like it spicier)

1 (8-oz [255-g]) package tempeh, cut into small cubes (or *use hemp tofu)

VEGETABLE LAYER

3–4 cups (450–600 g) chopped seasonal vegetables, such as julienned red bell pepper, sliced red or napa cabbage, thinly sliced carrot coins and cut green beans

EXTRAS

Fresh spinach

Sliced cucumbers

Bean sprouts

Extra Sriracha

Extra soy sauce

For the potato layer, add 1½ cups (355 ml) water to your Instant Pot, place a vegetable steamer on top and spread out the potatoes.

For the tempeh layer, add all the tempeh ingredients to a bowl and toss. Place in a Pyrex container, cover with foil and place on the potatoes.

For the vegetable layer, place the vegetables in a Pyrex container, cover with foil and place on top of the dish containing the tempeh.

Cook on high pressure for 10 minutes. Let the pressure release naturally. Once the pressure indicator goes down, remove the lid and carefully lift out the pans.

Serve by layering the tempeh and sauce over the potatoes and top with the steamed veggies. Let diners add the extras they want to their bowl.

PER SERVING: Calories 686.4, protein 30.6 g, total fat 40.0 g, carbohydrates 61.6 g, sodium 744.3 mg, fiber 11.4 g

I use a Pyrex 3-cup (700-ml) small rectangular pan for this. You can fit two on top of the rack and you can even store the leftovers right in the cooking containers! Be sure to take a look at "Accessory Resources" on page 209 for more ideas.

Technically, this recipe has no added refined oil, but we all know that coconut milk is high in fat. If you are on a no- or restricted-oil diet, you can always use unsweetened coconut milk from a carton, such as So Delicious, and a little coconut extract to get a similar flavor with fewer calories.

BLACK AS NIGHT LAYERED HALLOWEEN DINNER

gluten-free, soy-free, no added oil

Fall is one of my favorite seasons and Halloween is by far my favorite holiday. I even wrote a whole book of vegan Halloween recipes! The secret to a spooky dinner is a creative use of color while still making sure you have some great flavors. Black rice is actually great for you and is a whole grain, beluga lentils cook quickly and butternut squash paints on some bright colors. The cauliflower puree is the base for the sauce that ties it all together.

MAKES 4 SERVINGS

FORBIDDEN RICE LAYER

1½ cups (355 ml) water

1 cup (195 g) black forbidden rice

1 bouillon cube

LENTIL LAYER

1½ cups (355 ml) water

¾ cup (144 g) black beluga lentils

1 cup (140 g) diced butternut squash

1 bay leaf

½ tsp smoked paprika

⅛ tsp ground rosemary

CAULIFLOWER LAYER

2 cups (214 g) small cauliflower florets

BLENDER INGREDIENTS

¼ cup (60 ml) unsweetened nondairy milk

2 tbsp (10 g) nutritional yeast

½ tsp salt

½ cup (35 g) fresh spinach (optional)

Salt and pepper, to taste

For the rice layer, combine the 1½ cups (355 ml) water, forbidden rice and bouillon in your Instant Pot.

For the lentil layer, combine the 1½ cups (355 ml) water, lentils, squash and herbs in a 3-cup (700-ml) Pyrex container, cover with foil and place on top of the rice.

For the cauliflower layer, add the cauliflower to another Pyrex container, cover with foil and place on top of the dish containing the lentils.

Cook on high pressure for 15 minutes. Let the pressure release naturally. Once the pressure indicator goes down, remove the lid and carefully lift out the pans.

For the blender, add the cooked cauliflower, nondairy milk, nutritional yeast and salt to your blender and process until smooth. This will be your sauce. You can add ½ cup (35 g) fresh spinach to the blender and puree with the sauce to make a bright green sauce.

Before serving, add salt and pepper to taste to the lentil and butternut squash mixture.

Scoop a base of the black rice into bowls, spoon some of the creamy white sauce on top, then add the lentils, leaving a ring of sauce visible.

PER SERVING: Calories 258.6, protein 11.4 g, total fat 2.0 g, carbohydrates 50.6 g, sodium 29.2 mg, fiber 8.2 g

Don't wait for Halloween to serve this. Black rice has more fiber and less carbs than brown rice, but it gets its color from anthocyanin, which is an antioxidant.

CHEESY POTATO PIEROGIES (POLISH DUMPLINGS)

soy-free, no added oil

Once you've found where to get vegan dumpling wrappers there's no stopping you. Well, I've been pretty obsessed. Not only are they great for Asian dumplings, but you can also make ravioli with them as well as these decadent and comforting potato dumplings.

MAKES 12 PIEROGIES

POTATO FILLING

2 cups (300 g) chopped potato

½ cup (120 ml) unsweetened nondairy milk

3 tbsp (15 g) nutritional yeast

1 tsp dried dill

Salt and pepper, to taste

12 round vegan dumpling wrappers

TOPPINGS (OPTIONAL)

Cashew cream

Cauliflower Sour Cream (page 40)

Fresh dill

Sautéed onions

For the potato filling, add the chopped potatoes to your Instant Pot liner. Add water to cover and cook for 10 minutes on high pressure. Manually release the pressure and pour the potatoes into a strainer over the sink.

Put the drained potatoes in a bowl and mash. Mix in the nondairy milk, nutritional yeast and dill. Add salt and pepper to taste.

Cut out a round piece of parchment paper to fit inside a 6- or an 8-inch (15- or 20-cm) bamboo steamer. You will be able to fit all 12 dumplings in one level with the 8-inch (20-cm) one. No bamboo steamer? Just use your vegetable steamer coated with oil inside your Instant Pot.

Get a small bowl of water and set it up next to a cutting board to work on.

Place a wrapper on the cutting board and spread water around the edge of the wrapper with your fingertip. Add 1 tablespoon (15 g) filling to the middle of the wrapper and fold in half, matching the edges. Press them together. You can stop here or you can grab it by the middle of the sealed part and fold the dough in two places on either side. Then place in the steamer with the pleated side up.

Put the top on your bamboo steamer (if using) and add 1½ cups (355 ml) water and your rack to your Instant Pot. Then lower down the steamer.

Put the lid on and make sure that the vent is sealed. Select the steam setting and lower the time to 10 minutes.

Once they are cooked, open the steam release valve manually. Add your desired toppings.

PER PIEROGI: Calories 223.9, protein 7.2 g, total fat 0.7 g, carbohydrates 47.5 g, sodium 231.5 mg, fiber 2.9 g

CSA LAYERED INDIAN DINNER

gluten-free, soy-free, no added oil

I love my CSA, a weekly delivery of super-fresh vegetables right to my door. Of course, sometimes there are a few unusual root vegetables like kohlrabi, rutabaga and the like. This is the recipe to pull out for the odd root vegetable or old favorites like potatoes or beets.

MAKES 4 SERVINGS

YELLOW DAL LAYER

2 cups (475 ml) water

½ cup (96 g) yellow split peas, moong dal, red lentils or combination

2 tsp (8 g) grated ginger

1 tsp minced garlic

½ tsp ground cumin

½ tsp garam masala

¼ tsp ground turmeric

¼ tsp chili powder

⅛ tsp ground coriander

CURRIED ROOT VEGETABLE LAYER

2 cups (490 g) diced turnip, beet potato or other root vegetable

1 tbsp (15 ml) water

1 tbsp (6 g) finely shredded coconut

1 tsp crumbled curry leaves (dry or fresh) (optional)

½ tsp grated ginger

¼ tsp minced garlic

¼ tsp ground cumin

¼ tsp ground coriander

¼ tsp ground turmeric

¼ tsp garam masala

⅛ tsp chili powder

⅛ tsp fennel seeds

RICE LAYER

1 cup (185 g) brown basmati rice

1¼ cups (295 ml) water

BEFORE SERVING

Salt, to taste

For the yellow dal layer, add all the yellow dal ingredients directly to the Instant Pot liner, mix well and add the rack on top of that.

For the curried vegetable layer, add all the curried root vegetable ingredients to a short Pyrex container and toss. Place on the rack above the dal. (If you need to, you can wrap this layer in foil if you can't fit two Pyrex containers above the dal.)

For the rice layer, combine the rice and water together in a short Pyrex container and place, uncovered, on top of the root veggie layer.

Cook on high pressure for 40 minutes. Let the pressure release naturally. Once the pressure indicator goes down, remove the lid and carefully lift out the pans.

Before serving, taste each component and add salt to taste.

PER SERVING: Calories 142.7, protein 4.9 g, total fat 1.1 g, carbohydrates 28.7 g, sodium 15.9 mg, fiber 4.8 g

I use a Pyrex 3-cup (700-ml) small rectangular pan for this. You can fit two on top of the rack and you can even store the leftovers right in the cooking containers!

CREAMY MUSHROOM CURRY WITH BROWN BASMATI RICE PILAF

gluten-free, soy-free, no added oil

Here's a whole Indian meal made at the same time. The creamy mushroom and veggie curry is served over the subtly spiced basmati rice.

MAKES 2 SERVINGS

BROWN BASMATI RICE PILAF INGREDIENTS

1 cup (185 g) brown basmati rice

1½ cups (355 ml) water

1 cardamom pod

1 cinnamon stick

½ tsp cumin seeds

¼ tsp ground turmeric

¼ tsp salt

CREAMY MUSHROOM CURRY INGREDIENTS

1½ cups (108 g) sliced mushrooms

1 cup (128 g) cubed potatoes, cauliflower florets, carrots, sweet potato or combination

½ cup (120 ml) unsweetened nondairy milk

¼ cup (61 g) unsweetened plain vegan yogurt or cashew cream

1 tsp grated ginger

½ tsp minced garlic

½ tsp salt

½ tsp garam masala

¼ tsp ground turmeric

¼ tsp ground coriander

⅛ tsp chili powder

For the rice pilaf, combine the rice, water, cardamom pod, cinnamon stick, cumin seeds, turmeric and salt in your Instant Pot insert.

For the mushroom curry, get a Pyrex dish that fits into your Instant Pot, then mix the mushrooms, potatoes, milk, yogurt, ginger, garlic, salt, garam masala, turmeric, coriander and chili powder in it. Cover with foil.

If your pan does not fit inside the rack handles, you will need to fashion some handles out of aluminum foil to lower the pan into the cooker. Tear off two pieces of foil about 3 feet (1 m) long, fold each one lengthwise two times. Lay the foil handles out on the counter in a plus sign near your cooker. Place your pan in the center, where the two pieces cross. Pull the handles up and carefully lift the pan into your Instant Pot.

Cook on high pressure for 27 minutes.

Let the pressure release naturally. Once the pressure indicator goes down, remove the lid, lift out the pan using the foil handles and remove the foil that's covering the pan. Remove and discard the cardamom pod and cinnamon stick from the rice.

PER SERVING: Calories 207.7, protein 7.3 g, total fat 2.2 g, carbohydrates 40.5 g, sodium 667 mg, fiber 4.5 g

One of my testers used plain vegan yogurt that was not unsweetened and liked it just fine. Sometimes it can be hard to find unsweetened plain vegan yogurt, so you can try making your own soy yogurt on page 36.

SOUTHERN BREAKFAST

gluten-free, soy-free option*, no added oil

Some mornings call for a big breakfast, and this recipe gives you grits and a scramble all from one Instant Pot. If you have problems with your grits being lumpy, cook for 4 minutes and carefully release the pressure manually. Whisk the grits, then cook the additional 4 minutes on high pressure and let the pressure release naturally after the second cook.

MAKES 2 SERVINGS

GRITS LAYER

½ cup (85 g) grits or polenta

2¼ cups (535 ml) water

A few drops liquid smoke (optional, for smoky grits)

2–4 tbsp (10–20 g) nutritional yeast (optional, for cheesy grits)

½ tsp salt

¼ tsp black pepper, or to taste

SCRAMBLED TOFU LAYER

2 (12.3-oz [349-g]) aseptic boxes firm silken tofu or 1 (14-oz [397-g]) block extra-firm tofu (or regular tofu, pressed) (or *use 2 cups [500 g] mashed chickpeas)

2 tbsp (10 g) nutritional yeast

½–1 tsp kala namak (black salt)

½ tsp turmeric

⅛ tsp pepper

Optional veggies: minced or shredded onion, bell pepper, mushrooms or greens

For the grits layer, whisk together the grits, water, liquid smoke (if using), nutritional yeast (if using), salt and pepper in your Instant Pot insert.

For the scrambled tofu layer, in a bowl, mash together the tofu, nutritional yeast, kala namak, turmeric and pepper. Add any optional veggies you are using. Wrap in foil and lower on top of the grits. Cook on high pressure for 8 minutes.

Let the pressure release naturally. Once the pressure indicator goes down, remove the lid and lift out the foil packet carefully.

Mix the grits well. If they are sticking to the bottom, try scraping with a spatula and mixing. Serve on the side of the tofu scramble.

PER SERVING: Calories 343.3, protein 28.7 g, total fat 8.7 g, carbohydrates 40.4 g, sodium 24.0 mg, fiber 5.4 g

If you don't like cooking with foil on top of your grits, you can cook the grits in a large Pyrex bowl that fits in your Instant Pot and balance the foil packet on top of that. Also, you can wrap the tofu mixture in parchment paper and then wrap that in foil. You will need to add 1½ cups (355 ml) water and the rack that came with your Instant Pot. Cook on high pressure for 13 minutes and let the pressure release naturally.

CHAPTER 8

Decadent and Healthy Desserts

What's a fun appliance without some sweets to make in it, too? All of these desserts have options for no added oil, and some sugar-free options, too.

Make some vanilla spice tea to have with a slice of Zucchini Lemon Spelt Snack Cake on page 32 or Chocolate Tofu Cheesecake on page 202. You are going to love making sweets in your Instant Pot.

VANILLA SPICE TEA CONCENTRATE

gluten-free*, soy-free, no added oil

I love having a pitcher of infused tea concentrate in my fridge when I wake up in the morning. It's so much cheaper to make it yourself, and you can customize the spices to your liking. Note: There is no nutritional data for this recipe as it would depend on your choice of sweetener (if using).

MAKES ABOUT 8 CUPS (1.9 L)

8 cups (1.9 L) water

30 whole allspice berries

22 green cardamom pods

12 whole cloves

8 cinnamon sticks

3" (7.5-cm) piece fresh ginger, sliced or chopped

2 whole star anise

4 family-sized tea bags or 8 regular-sized tea bags (You can use black, rooibos or green tea. Just steep according to the directions on the tea you use.)

1 tbsp (15 ml) pure vanilla extract

Sweetener of choice, to taste

Add everything but the tea bags, vanilla and sweetener to your Instant Pot. Put the lid on and make sure the steam release handle is set to sealing, or closed. Select the manual setting and set to cook for 5 minutes.

The Instant Pot timer will begin counting down the time once it gets up to pressure. Allow the pressure to release naturally. You'll know when it's ready because the round silver pressure gauge will drop down.

Once the gauge drops down, remove the lid, add the tea bags and steep for 4 minutes.

Remove the tea bags and pour through a strainer into the pitcher you will store the concentrate in. Mix in the vanilla extract and sweetener to taste. You can leave it unsweetened if you'd prefer.

Store in the fridge for up to 10 days.

HOW TO USE THE CONCENTRATE
Add equal parts nondairy milk and tea concentrate, then either heat it up or serve over ice. I love to use unsweetened vanilla almond milk with this recipe.

TRES LECHES-INSPIRED DESSERT TAMALE

gluten-free, soy-free, no added oil option*

Don't panic, there's only nondairy milk in these caramel-y coconut tamales. They are stuffed with a date caramel filling and covered in a sweet coconut milk sauce. This is a wow dessert that's actually pretty easy to make. It's also a magical ending to a tamale dinner party! (You can easily double the Tamales Made with Coconut Oil [page 106] recipe if you want to make more.)

MAKES 12 TAMALES

1 recipe Tamales Made with Coconut Oil (page 106) or *Oil-Free Pumpkin Tamales (page 102)

12 corn husks

Date Caramel Filling (recipe follows)

Creamy Coconut Sauce (page 118)

Put a steamer or mesh insert into your Instant Pot and add 1½ cups (355 ml) water.

Set up a workstation with a cutting board, the tamale batter and corn husks. Put ⅓ cup (80 ml) tamale batter in the top half of the corn husk and spread into a thin rectangle that goes to the top (or wide part) of the husk. I do this with a spatula so that I can scrape the dough into the shape I want. In the middle add 1 tablespoon (15 g) filling.

Fold the pointed end up to the top, fold one side over the other and tightly roll it into a flat tube. Place with the open side up in the steamer and repeat until all the batter is used. Cook on high pressure for 20 minutes and let the pressure release naturally. Serve topped with the Creamy Coconut Sauce.

PER TAMALE, NO FILLING OR SAUCE: Calories 187.0, protein 0.4 g, total fat 14.3 g, carbohydrates 14.6 g, sodium 41.6 mg, fiber 0.0 g

DATE CARAMEL FILLING

MAKES ABOUT 4 CUPS (940 G)

3 cups (700 ml) water

1 (7-oz [227-g]) package pitted dates

2 tsp (10 ml) pure vanilla extract

Add the water and dates to your Instant Pot. Cook on high pressure for 10 minutes and let the pressure release naturally. Using tongs or a slotted spoon, carefully transfer the dates to your blender. Add the vanilla and cooking water as needed to puree the dates into a paste.

Store in the fridge. This is great in coffee, as a dip for apple slices and much more. You will have leftovers to play with if you only make 12 tamales.

PER ¼-CUP (60 G) SERVING, FILLING ONLY: Calories 41.5, protein 0.3 g, total fat 0.1 g, carbohydrates 10.7 g, sodium 1.2 mg, fiber 1.1 g

SALTED DATE CARAMEL TAPIOCA PUDDING

gluten-free, soy-free, no added oil

I think you're either a tapioca lover or you aren't. Me, I adore the stuff. I eat it cold from the fridge, which is perfect for a hot summer day. This recipe is fancied up with some date caramel from page 197 and a little salt. I like my tapioca pudding thick, but you can always stir in more milk after it's cooked if you like yours thinner.

MAKES 6 SERVINGS

2 cups (475 ml) unsweetened nondairy milk (plain or vanilla)

½ cup (76 g) small tapioca pearls

½ cup (120 g) Date Caramel Filling (page 197)

1 tsp pure vanilla extract

Salt, to taste

Add the nondairy milk, tapioca and date caramel to your Instant Pot. Cook on high pressure for 8 minutes. Let the pressure release naturally. Don't worry if the pudding is thinner than you expect. It will thicken more in the fridge.

Stir in the vanilla and salt to taste. Pour into a storage container and put in the fridge for at least 4 hours before serving.

Fancy it up and top each portion with vegan chocolate curls or a sprinkle of kosher salt.

PER SERVING: Calories 94.5, protein 3.1 g, total fat 1.5 g, carbohydrates 16.6 g, sodium 10.6 mg, fiber 1.8 g

Use this as a base to create your own special tapioca recipe. Use the sweetener of your choice, to taste, and add extracts and herbs. Here are a few combos that I suggest: thyme and lemon, lavender chocolate, vanilla and orange flower pistachio.

HOLIDAY ORANGE SPICE CAKE

gluten-free option*, soy-free, no added oil option**

Spice cake is good anytime of the year, but I crave it at the holidays. This cake is super moist because it's steamed and reminds me a little of an English steamed pudding. You can vary the dried fruit and nuts to match what you have in your pantry.

MAKES 6 SERVINGS

DRY INGREDIENTS

1¼ cups (150 g) whole wheat pastry flour (or *use a gluten-free baking mix)

1½ tsp (4 g) ground cinnamon

1 tsp ground allspice

½ tsp baking soda

½ tsp baking powder

¼ tsp ground cloves

WET INGREDIENTS

½ cup (120 ml) orange juice with pulp (about 1 medium orange)

⅓ cup (80 ml) maple syrup or agave nectar

2 tbsp (14 g) ground flaxseed

3 tbsp (41 g) melted coconut oil (or **use applesauce)

MIX-INS

2 tbsp (12 g) orange zest (or 1 tsp orange extract)

¾ cup (75 g) dried cranberries or diced dried dates

½ cup (55 g) chopped walnuts or pecans

Oil a 6- or 7-inch (15- or 17.5-cm) Bundt pan and set aside.

For the dry ingredients, mix the flour, cinnamon, allspice, baking soda, baking powder and cloves in a medium-size mixing bowl.

For the wet ingredients, combine the juice, syrup, flaxseed and oil in a large measuring cup. Add the wet ingredients to the dry and mix well. Fold in the mix-ins.

Spread the cake mixture into your prepared pan and cover with foil.

Put the steel insert into your Instant Pot, pour in 1½ cups (355 ml) water and add the stainless steel steam rack with handles that came with your Instant Pot.

If your pan does not fit inside the rack handles, you will need to fashion some handles out of aluminum foil to lower the pan into the cooker. Tear off two pieces of foil about 3 feet (1 m) long, fold each one lengthwise two times. Lay the foil handles out on the counter in a plus sign near your cooker. Place your pan in the center, where the two pieces cross. Pull the handles up and carefully lift the pan into your Instant Pot.

Place the lid on with the steam release handle set to sealing, or closed; cook on high pressure for 35 minutes. Let the pressure release naturally.

Once the pressure indicator goes down, remove the lid, lift out the pan using the foil handles and remove the foil that's covering the pan.

Let cool so that it cuts easier; it will crumble if cut warm.

PER SERVING: Calories 332.1, protein 4.8 g, total fat 15.0 g, carbohydrates 48.5 g, sodium 148.3 mg, fiber 5.9 g

You can get crazy with other dried fruit, spices, nuts and even some candied ginger!

CHOCOLATE TOFU CHEESECAKE WITH A HAZELNUT-OAT CRUST

gluten-free*, no added oil

This is a decadent sweet treat that's actually low in sugar. It's a thick, New York–style cheesecake with a base of silken tofu. It's sweetened with stevia, but it does have a tiny bit of maple syrup to round out the mouthfeel.

MAKES 8 SERVINGS

CRUST INGREDIENTS

1 cup (115 g) hazelnuts

1 cup (92 g) rolled oats (*make sure the oats are labeled gluten-free)

¼ cup (22 g) cocoa powder

¼ tsp salt

15 drops vanilla-flavored stevia

3 tbsp (45 ml) unsweetened vanilla-flavored nondairy milk

1 tbsp (15 ml) maple syrup or agave nectar

FILLING INGREDIENTS

2 (12.3-oz [349-g]) boxes silken tofu

3 oz (84 g) unsweetened baking chocolate, melted

20 drops vanilla-flavored stevia

¼ cup (22 g) cocoa powder

2 tbsp (16 g) arrowroot powder

1 tbsp (15 ml) maple syrup or agave nectar

1 tsp pure vanilla extract

¼ tsp salt

For the crust, preheat your oven to 350°F (180°C, or gas mark 4). Place the hazelnuts on a baking sheet and toast for 5 minutes, or until they become fragrant and lightly browned. Let cool, then rub the hazelnuts in a lint-free cloth to remove the dark skins. Add the hazelnuts, oats, cocoa powder and salt to your food processor and process until finely ground. Add the stevia, nondairy milk and maple syrup and process until it is mixed well. It should be moist enough to stick together; add an additional tablespoon (15 ml) nondairy milk if it won't hold together.

Oil a 7-inch (17.5-cm) springform pan that fits into your Instant Pot, or use a cake pan with a removable bottom that is 8 inches (20 cm) or smaller. Press the crust mixture evenly across the bottom of the pan.

For the filling, add the tofu, melted chocolate and stevia to your blender and blend until silky smooth. You will need to scrape down the blender and blend again a few times to get it that consistency. Add the cocoa powder, arrowroot powder, maple syrup, vanilla and salt to the blender mixture and blend again until smooth. Pour this over the crust and use an offset spatula to smooth the top evenly. Cover with foil.

Put the steel insert into your Instant Pot, add 1½ cups (355 ml) water to the bottom and add the stainless steel steam rack with handles that came with your Instant Pot. You will need to fashion some handles out of aluminum foil to lower the pan full of cheesecake into the cooker. Tear off two pieces of foil about 3 feet (1 m) long, fold each one lengthwise two times. Lay the foil handles out on the counter in a plus sign near your cooker. Place your pan in the center, where the two pieces cross. Pull the handles up and carefully lift the pan into your Instant Pot.

Place the lid on with the steam release handle closed and cook on high pressure for 20 minutes. Let the pressure release naturally. Once the pressure indicator goes down, remove the lid, lift out the pan using the foil handles and remove the foil that's covering the pan. Once the pan is cool enough to touch, either place in the freezer for an hour or in the fridge for at least 4 hours to set. Remove the ring and serve.

PER SERVING: Calories 238.2, protein 8.8 g, total fat 16.7 g, carbohydrates 21.4 g, sodium 228.8 mg, fiber 6.3 g

SPICED OAT-STUFFED APPLES

gluten-free*, soy-free, no added oil

What's better than a bowl of oats in the morning? An apple full of oats, that's what! These are great for breakfast and dessert. Be aware that some apples are denser than others and may require a longer cooking time. Honestly, I just use whatever I have, but I don't mind if the apples keep some of their bite.

MAKES 4 SERVINGS (8 APPLE HALVES)

1 cup (92 g) rolled oats (*make sure the oats are labeled gluten-free)

¼ cup (60 ml) maple syrup

1 tbsp (7 g) ground flaxseed

1 tbsp (15 ml) spiced rum (or 1 tsp pure vanilla extract)

1 tsp ground cinnamon

Pinch of ground cloves

Pinch of salt

4 medium apples, cored and cut in half vertically

Mix the oats, maple syrup, flaxseed, spiced rum, cinnamon, cloves and salt in a bowl.

Place a rack in your Instant Pot and pour in 1½ cups (355 ml) water.

Using about 2 tablespoons (20 g) of the filling, cover the cut side of the apple and press the mixture down into the cavity. Place in a pan that fits in your Instant Pot. Repeat with each apple half. Cover the dish with foil and place in the Instant Pot.

Cook on high pressure for 30 minutes and let the pressure release naturally. If your apples aren't easily pierced with a fork, put the lid back on and cook for another 15–25 minutes.

PER SERVING: Calories 214.4, protein 3.2 g, total fat 2.3 g, carbohydrates 46.3 g, sodium 1.8 mg, fiber 5.8 g

I like this with all types of apples, including some that don't soften as much with cooking. One of my testers likes her apples softer and recommends that you use Granny Smith.

APPENDIXES

RECIPE LIST BY COURSE

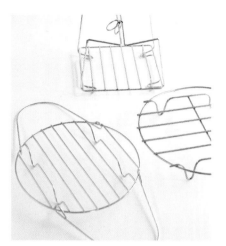

Cooking racks

Metal steam baskets

Silicone steamer baskets

Bento steamer

3 cup (710 g) Pyrex baking dishes

Oven safe dishes

Stackable stainless stacking pans with lids

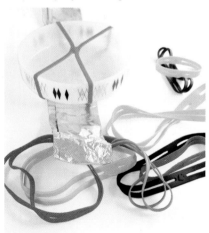

Silicone bands

Pan grabbers

ACCESSORY RESOURCES

There are many accessories you can use in your Instant Pot to increase what you can cook in it and how many things you can cook at one time.

Your Instant Pot comes with a handy rack to use, but you can get extra racks online or at Asian markets so that you can use more than one to stack ovenproof containers on.

You can also use a vegetable steamer in place of a rack or use as it was intended, to steam things. Bamboo steamers also work great in the Instant Pot; just make sure you buy a size that will fit inside!

The ovenproof containers that you stack can be fancy stainless steel pots that stack together in their own rack or ovenproof Pyrex and ceramic dishes—even tea cups and ramekins will work.

For my layered meals, I often cook something under the rack that comes with the Instant Pot and stack two 3-cup (700-g) rectangular Pyrex containers on top of each other so I can cook three recipes at once.

You can also use silicone pans, and rubber band–type silicone bands can be used as a way to easily remove cooking vessels, or you can make handles with simple aluminum foil.

Another extra that's nice to have are plate retriever tongs or little silicone covers for your fingertips. This helps you get out pans that you've stacked or even get the stainless steel insert out without burning yourself.

You can get links to my favorite accessories on my blog at HealthySlowCooking.com/instantpotaccessories.

RECOMMENDED READING

FACEBOOK GROUPS

Eat to Live Instant Pot Users Group
www.facebook.com/groups/InstaPotUsersETL

Instant Pot Vegan Recipes
www.facebook.com/groups/InstantPotVeganRecipes

Instant Pot Community (not vegan)
www.facebook.com/groups/InstantPotCommunity

Plant-Based Instant Pot People
www.facebook.com/groups/790787064328258

WEBSITES AND BLOGS

Vegan Pressure Cooker

healthyslowcooking.com

fatfreevegan.com

glueandglitter.com

jlgoesvegan.com

theveggiequeen.com

Non-Vegan Pressure Cooker

HipPressureCooking.com

PressureCookingToday.com

OTHER COOKBOOKS

Vegan Pressure Cooker

Vegan Under Pressure by Jill Nussinow

Vegan Pressure Cooking by JL Fields

O M Gee Good! Instant Pot Meals, Plant-Based & Oil-Free by Jill McKeever

The New Fast Food by Jill Nussinow

Non-Vegan Pressure Cooker

Hip Pressure Cooking by Laura D.A. Pazzaglia

Great Vegetarian Cooking Under Pressure by Lorna J. Sass

Non-Pressure Cooker Vegan

OATrageous Oatmeals by Kathy Hester

The Great Vegan Bean Book by Kathy Hester

The Easy Vegan Cookbook by Kathy Hester

Vegan Pizza by Julie Hasson

ACKNOWLEDGMENTS

This is my third book with Page Street Publishing. I adore working with Will Kiester and his supportive team. Lisa and Sally Ekus are the best agents a girl could ever hope for and were a wonderful support throughout the whole process of this book. Thank you all so much for believing in my vision.

I have so much gratitude for my testers' help and guidance: Rochelle Arvizo, Mary Banker, Kimber Cherry, Dorian Farrow, Brandie Faust, Michelle L. Imber, Amy Katz, Sarah Limacher, Ann Oliverio, Jenna Patton, Dianne Wenz and Ruth Zagg.

Many thanks to Marissa Giambelluca and Karen Levy for doing an amazing editing job.

Thank you to Kylie Alexander for the wonderful layout. As usual, I can't possibly thank Cheryl Purser enough, and you can thank her for the nutritionals in this book.

ABOUT THE AUTHOR

Kathy Hester is the author of *The Easy Vegan Cookbook, OATrageous Oatmeals, The Great Vegan Bean Book* and the best-selling *The Vegan Slow Cooker*. She's the blogger behind HealthySlowCooking.com, does freelance writing, food styling, food photography and recipe development, and teaches people just how easy it is to cook.

When she's not writing or being a mad scientist in the kitchen, she's probably drinking tea on the deck while reading *Harry Potter* one more time.

She lives in Durham, North Carolina, with a grown-up picky eater, two quirky dogs and two grumpy cats.

INDEX